Henry H. Hadley

Rescue Songs by One Hundred Popular Composers and Gifted Song Writers

Specially fitted for rescue missions and meetings, rescue workers and evangelists, and revival services

Henry H. Hadley

Rescue Songs by One Hundred Popular Composers and Gifted Song Writers
Specially fitted for rescue missions and meetings, rescue workers and evangelists, and revival services

ISBN/EAN: 9783337386191

Printed in Europe, USA, Canada, Australia, Japan

Cover: Foto ©Thomas Meinert / pixelio.de

More available books at **www.hansebooks.com**

BY

ONE HUNDRED POPULAR COMPOSERS

AND

GIFTED SONG WRITERS

SPECIALLY FITTED FOR

RESCUE MISSIONS AND MEETINGS
RESCUE WORKERS AND EVANGELISTS
AND REVIVAL SERVICES

COMPILED BY

COL. HENRY H. HADLEY

NEW YORK
PUBILSHED FOR THE CHRISTIAN MEN'S UNION
433 LEXINGTON AVENUE

Copyright, 1890, by H. H. HADLEY
Copyright, 1893, by H. H. HADLEY

The compiler has dedicated in this book, several selections to friends who have assisted, and in memory of others.

PREFACE.

There are more songs suitable for *rescue work* in RESCUE SONGS than in any other book, including the best from almost every source.

Many publishers, writers and composers donated the pieces asked for, and others sold them at reasonable rates.

But for this and the important fact that several hundred dollars with which to buy the music and make the plates, were contributed by good friends of missions and of rescue work, this book would have to be sold at the usual price for such books, say 35 to 50 cents per copy. Thanks to these friends, the publishers are now enabled to furnish RESCUE SONGS within the means of the poorest mission, church or Sunday-school. The thanks of all rescue workers are due to those who have made it possible to give so good a book a wide circulation where so much needed. To each one who has helped or prayed for this cheery messenger of hope and peace, is tendered (In His Name) the sincere thanks of   H. H. H.

Please pray that this copy may be the means of saving some soul. See MATT. 15: 19 and 1 JOHN 1: 7.

C. H. WOODMAN, MUSIC TYPOGRAPHER, 144 HANOVER ST., BOSTON

RESCUE SONGS.

1. O Could I Speak the Matchless Worth.

SAMUEL MEDLEY.   Arr. by LOWELL MASON.

1. O could I speak the match-less worth, O could I sound
   the glo-ries forth, Which in my Sav-iour shine, I'd soar and
   touch the heavenly strings, And vie with Ga-briel while He sings
   In notes al-most di-vine, In notes al-most di-vine.

2. I'd sing the pre-cious blood He spilt, My ran-som from
   the dread-ful guilt Of sin, and wrath di-vine; I'd sing His
   glo-rious right-eous-ness, In which all-per-fect, heaven-ly dress
   My soul shall ev-er shine, My soul shall ev-er shine.

3. I'd sing the char-ac-ters He bears, And all the forms
   of love He wears, Ex-alt-ed on His throne; In loft-iest
   songs of sweet-est praise, I would to ev-er-last-ing days
   Make all His glo-ries known, Make all His glo-ries known.

4. Well, the de-light-ful day will come When my dear Lord
   will bring me home, And I shall see His face; Then with my
   Sav-iour, Broth-er, Friend, A blest e-ter-ni-ty I'll spend.
   Tri-umph-ant in His grace, Tri-umph-ant in His grace.

2. The Great Physician.

REV. WM. HUNTER.   Arr. by REV. J. H. STOCKTON.

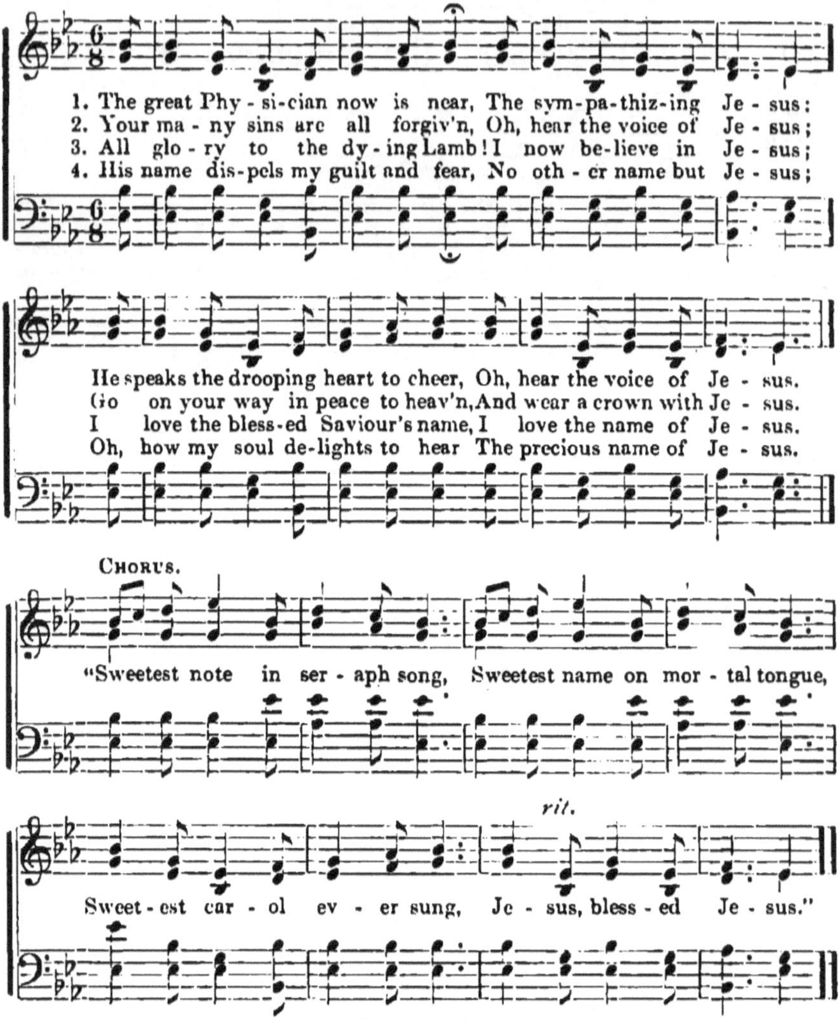

1. The great Physician now is near, The sympathizing Jesus;
He speaks the drooping heart to cheer, Oh, hear the voice of Jesus.
2. Your many sins are all forgiv'n, Oh, hear the voice of Jesus;
Go on your way in peace to heav'n, And wear a crown with Jesus.
3. All glory to the dying Lamb! I now believe in Jesus;
I love the blessed Saviour's name, I love the name of Jesus.
4. His name dispels my guilt and fear, No other name but Jesus;
Oh, how my soul delights to hear The precious name of Jesus.

CHORUS.

"Sweetest note in seraph song, Sweetest name on mortal tongue, Sweetest carol ever sung, Jesus, blessed Jesus."

By permission.

3. Burst, Ye Emerald Gates.

1 Burst, ye emerald gates, and bring
   To my raptured vision
All th' ecstatic joys that spring
   Round the bright elysian.
Lo! we lift our longing eyes,
Break! ye intervening skies,
Sons of righteousness, arise,
Ope' the gates of Paradise.

2 Hark! the thrilling symphonies,
   Seem methinks to seize us,
Join we in the holy lays,
   Jesus came to save us:
Sweetest sound in seraph's song,
Sweetest note on mortal tongue,
Sweetest carol ever sung,
Let its echoes flow along.

4. A Shout in the Camp.

Dedicated to Arthur L. Robinson.

FANNY J. CROSBY. — JNO. R. SWENEY.

1. There's a shout in the camp, for the Lord is here, Hal-le-lu-jah! praise His name; To the feast of His love we again draw near, Praise, oh, praise His name.
2. There's a shout in the camp like the shout of old, Hal-le-lu-jah! praise His name; For the cloud of His glo-ry we now be-hold, Praise, oh, praise His name.
3. There's a shout in the ranks of the King of kings, Hal-le-lu-jah! praise His name; While we drink at the Rock from the living springs, Praise, oh, praise His name.
4. There's a shout in the camp while our souls re-peat Hal-le-lu-jah! praise His name; There is room for the world at the Saviour's feet, Praise, oh, praise His name.

CHORUS.

Room for the millions! room for all! Hal-le-lu-jah! praise His name; Come to the banquet, great and small, Praise, oh, praise His name.

From "Precious Hymns," by permission of JOHN. J. HOOD.

5. Jesus Shall Reign.

H. C. ZEUNER.

1. Jesus shall reign where'er the sun Does His suc-ces-sive jour-neys run;
2. For Him shall endless prayer be made, And endless praises crown His head;
3. People and realms of every tongue Dwell on His love with sweetest song;
4. Blessings abound where'er He reigns; The prisoner leaps to lose his chains;
5. Let ev-ery creat-ure rise and bring Pe - cu-liar hon - ors to their King:

His kingdom stretch from shore to shore, Till moons shall wax and wane no more.
His name, like sweet perfume, shall rise With every morning sac - ri - fice.
And in-fant voi - ces shall proclaim The early blessings on His name.
The wea - ry find e - ter-nal rest, And all the sons of want are blest.
An - gels de-scend with songs a-gain, And earth repeat the loud A - men!

6. Hebron. L. M.

ISAAC WATTS.   LOWELL MASON.

1. Thus far the Lord hath led me on, Thus far His power prolongs my days;
2. Much of my time has run to waste, And I, per-haps, am near my home;
3. I lay my bod - y down to sleep; Peace is the pil - low for my head;
4. Thus, when the night of death shall come, My flesh shall rest beneath the ground,

And every evening shall make known Some fresh me-mo-rial of His grace.
But He forgives my follies past, And gives me strength for days to come.
While well-appointed angels keep Their watchful stations round my bed.
And wait Thy voice to rouse my tomb, With sweet sal-va-tion in the sound.

10. My Country! 'tis of Thee.

SAMUEL F. SMITH.   HENRY CAREY.

1. My country! 'tis of thee, Sweet land of liberty, Of thee I sing: Land where my fathers died! Land of the pilgrims' pride! From every mountain side Let freedom ring!
2. My native country, thee, Land of the noble, free, Thy name I love; I love thy rocks and rills, Thy woods and templed hills: My heart with rapture thrills Like that above.
3. Let music swell the breeze, And ring from all the trees Sweet freedom's song: Let mortal tongues awake; Let all that breathe partake; Let rocks their silence break, The sound prolong.
4. Our fathers' God! to Thee, Author of liberty, To Thee we sing: Long may our land be bright With freedom's holy light; Protect us by Thy might, Great God, our King!

---

1 My faith looks up to Thee,
  Thou Lamb of Calvary,
    Saviour divine;
  Now hear me while I pray,
  Take all my guilt away,
  O let me from this day
    Be wholly Thine.

2 May Thy rich grace impart
  Strength to my fainting heart,
    My zeal inspire;
  As Thou hast died for me,
  O may my love to Thee
  Pure, warm, and changeless be,—
    A living fire.

3 While life's dark maze I tread,
  And griefs around me spread,
    Be Thou my guide;
  Bid darkness turn to day,
  Wipe sorrow's tears away,
  Nor let me ever stray
    From Thee aside.

4 When ends life's transient dream,
  When death's cold, sullen stream
    Shall o'er me roll,
  Blest Saviour, then, in love,
  Fear and distrust remove;
  O bear me safe above,—
    A ransomed soul.

RAY PALMER.

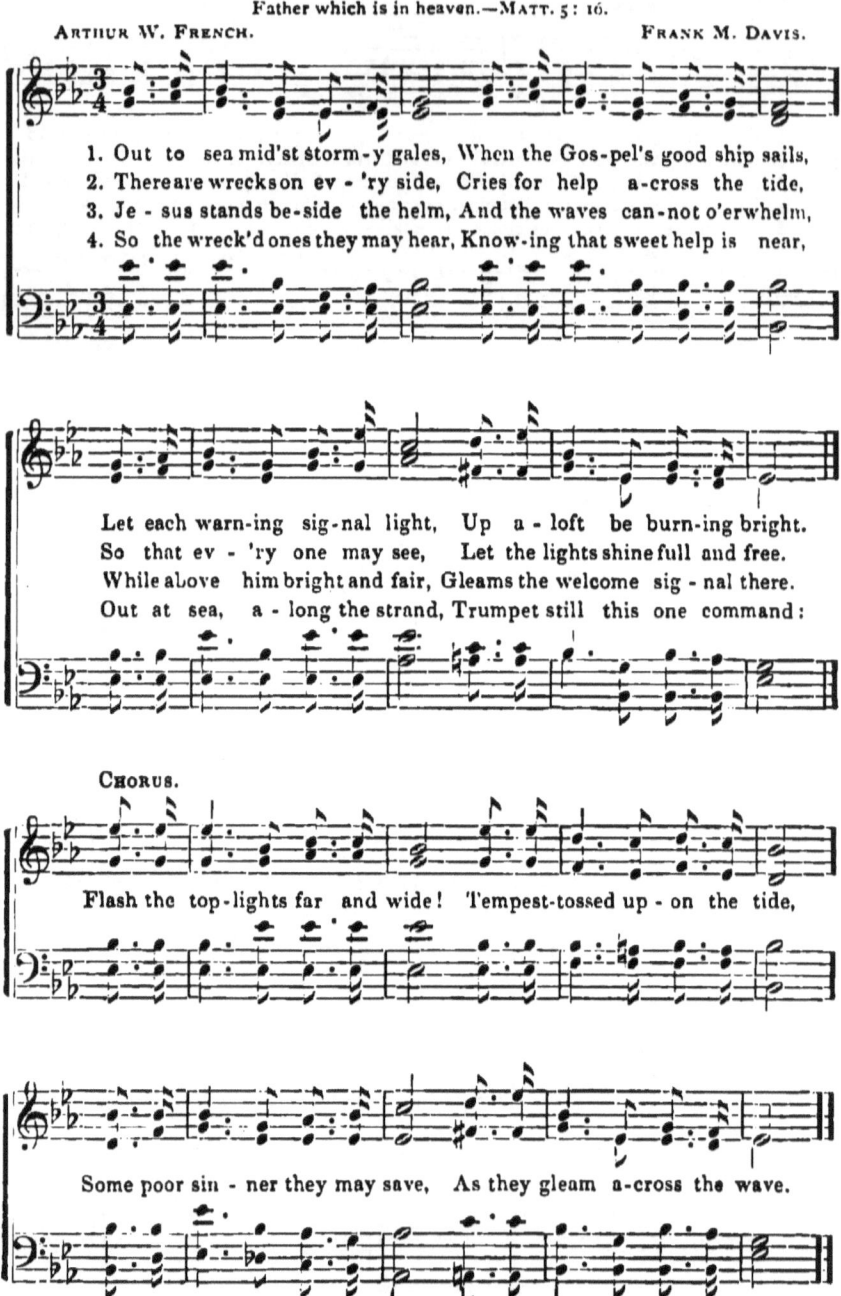

13. The Gospel Feast.

CHARLES WESLEY. "Come, for all things are ready."
Chorus by H. L. G.   LUKE 14: 16.   H. L. GILMOUR. By per.

1. Come, sinners, to the gospel feast; It is for you, it is for me;
   Let every soul be Jesus' guest; It is for you, it is for me.
2. Ye need not one be left behind, It is for you, it is for me;
   For God hath bidden all mankind, It is for you, it is for me.

D.S.—O weary wand'rer, come and see, It is for you, it is for me.

CHORUS.
Salvation full, salvation free, The price was paid on Calvary;

3 Sent by my Lord, on you I call;
  The invitation is to all:

4 Come, all the world! come, sinner, thou!
  All things in Christ are ready now.

5 Come, all ye souls by sin oppressed,
  Ye restless wanderers after rest;

6 Ye poor, and maimed, and halt, and blind,
  In Christ a hearty welcome find.

7 My message as from God receive;
  Ye all may come to Christ and live:

8 O let this love your hearts constrain,
  Nor suffer Him to die in vain.

9 See Him set forth before your eyes,
  That precious, bleeding sacrifice:

10 His offered benefits embrace,
   And freely now be saved by grace.

Copyright, 1889, by H. L. GILMOUR.

14. God's Word.
TUNE 13.

1 How precious is the book divine,
    By inspiration given;
  Bright as a lamp its teachings shine,
    To guide our souls to heaven.

2 Its light, descending from above,
    Our gloomy world to cheer,
  Displays a Saviour's boundless love,
    And brings His glories near.

3 It shows to man his wandering ways,
    And where his feet have trod;
  And brings to view the matchless grace
    Of a forgiving God.

4 My soul rejoices to pursue
    The steps of Him I love,
  Till glory breaks upon my view,
    In brighter worlds above.

15. The General Roll Call.

Mrs. Harriet E. Jones. — Frank M. Davis.

1. At the sounding of the trum-pet That shall sum-mon one and all
2. At the great and fi-nal judgment When all se-crets shall be known,
3. When we hear the gen-'ral roll call, Thro' the cit-y of the King,

To the throne of the E-ter-nal, Shall we trem-ble at the call?
To the ma-ny gathered millions That shall stand be-fore the throne,
And the ransomed ones re-joic-ing, Till the heavenly arch-es ring,

Shall we stand be-fore our Mak-er, In the rai-ment pure and white?
Shall we face the host of heav-en, And the bless-ed Lamb of God,
Shall we help to swell the mu-sic, Join the ev-er-last-ing strain?

Or go sad-ly from His presence To the realms of end-less night.
With our sinnings all for-giv-en Thro' the precious, precious blood?
Or go forth to death and darkness, There to ev-er-more re-main.

CHORUS.

O be read-y for the roll call, O be read-y for the roll call,

Copyright, 1893, by H. H. Hadley.

21. We Walk by Faith.

Words by FANNY J. CROSBY.   *Used by permission.*   Music by WM. J. KIRKPATRICK.

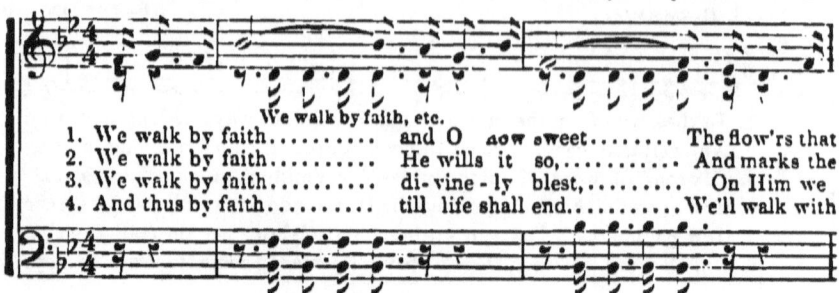

We walk by faith, etc.
1. We walk by faith............ and O now sweet.......... The flow'rs that
2. We walk by faith.......... He wills it so,............ And marks the
3. We walk by faith.......... di-vine-ly blest,.......... On Him we
4. And thus by faith.......... till life shall end.......... We'll walk with

grow........ beneath our feet...... And fragrance breathe.... a-long the
path........ that we should go;..... And when, at times....... our sky is
lean,........ in Him we rest;..... The more we trust........ our Shepherd's
Him,........ our dearest Friend,... Till safe we tread....... the fields of

way......... That leads the soul.......... to end-less day........
dim,......... He gent-ly draws........... us close to Him.......
care,......... The more His love........... 'tis ours to share.......
light,......... Where faith is lost............ in per'-fect sight.......

CHORUS.   *express.*

We walk by faith, but not a-lone, Our Shepherd's ten-der voice we hear,

Copyright, 1885, by W. J. Kirkpatrick.

We Walk by Faith. Concluded.

And feel His hand within our own, And know that He is al-ways near.

22. O Happy Day.

July 28th, 1886, 9.40 p. m. At the old Jerry McAuley Mission, 316 Water St., N. Y.
PHILIP DODDRIDGE.

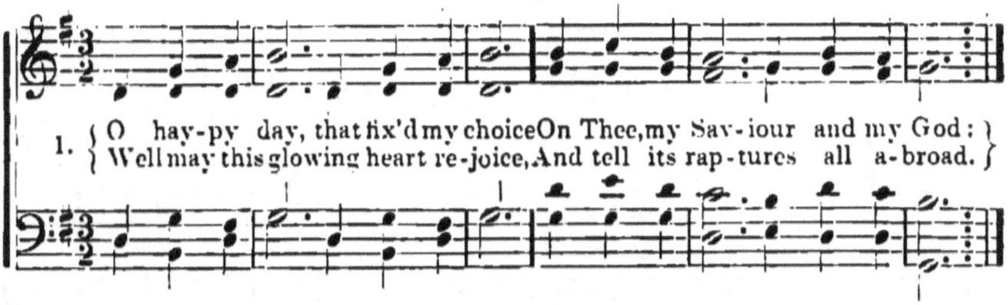

1. { O hap-py day, that fix'd my choice On Thee, my Sav-iour and my God: }
   { Well may this glowing heart re-joice, And tell its rap-tures all a-broad. }

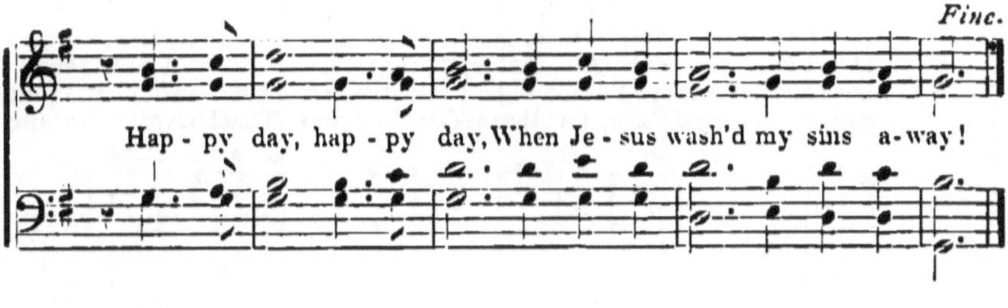

Hap-py day, hap-py day, When Je-sus wash'd my sins a-way!

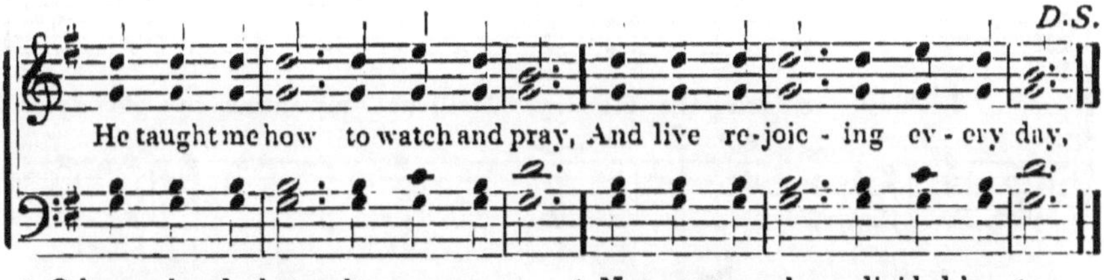

He taught me how to watch and pray, And live re-joic-ing ev-ery day,

2 O happy bond, that seals my vows
    To Him who merits all my love!
  Let cheerful anthems fill His house,
    While to that sacred shrine I move.

3 'Tis done! the great transaction's done!
    I am my Lord's, and He is mine:
  He drew me, and I follow'd on,
    Charmed to confess the voice divine.

4 Now rest, my long-divided heart;
    Fix'd on this blissful centre, rest;
  Nor ever from thy Lord depart;
    With Him, of every good possessed.

5 High Heaven that heard the solemn vow,
    That vow renew'd shall daily hear,
  Till in life's latest hour I bow,
    And bless in death a bond so dear.

24. The Pilgrim Company.

Arr. by Rev. W. McDonald.

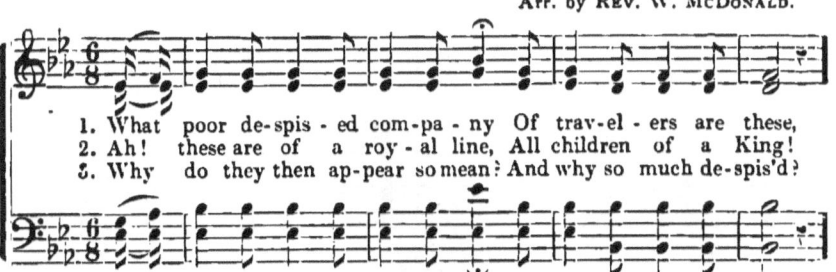

1. What poor despisèd company Of travelers are these,
2. Ah! these are of a royal line, All children of a King!
3. Why do they then appear so mean? And why so much despis'd?

Chorus.—I had rather be the least of them, Who are the Lord's alone,

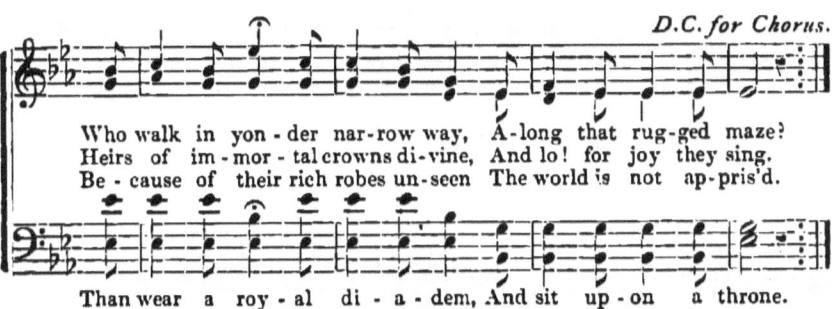

Who walk in yonder narrow way, Along that rugged maze?
Heirs of immortal crowns divine, And lo! for joy they sing.
Because of their rich robes unseen The world is not appris'd.

Than wear a royal diadem, And sit upon a throne.

And sit upon a throne, And sit upon a throne;

Than wear a royal diadem, And sit upon a throne.

4 But some of them seem poor, distress'd,
And lacking daily bread:
Ah! they're of boundless wealth possess'd,
With heavenly manna fed.

5 Why do they shun the pleasing path
That worldlings love so well?
Because it is the way to death:
The open road to hell.

6 But why keep they the narrow road,
That rugged thorny maze?
Why, that's the way their Leader trod;
They love and keep His ways.

7 What, is there then no other road
To Salem's happy ground?
Christ is the only way to God:
None other can be found.

27. Rejoice and be Glad.

Rev. Horatius Bonar, 1874.   English Melody.

1. Rejoice and be glad! The Redeemer has come! Go look on His cra-dle,
2. Rejoice and be glad! It is sunshine at last! The clouds have departed,
3. Rejoice and be glad! For the blood hath been shed; Redemption is finish'd,

CHORUS.

His cross and His tomb. Sound His prais-es, tell the sto-ry Of
The shad-ows are past.
The price hath been paid.

Him who was slain; Sound His praises, tell with gladness He liv-eth a-gain.

last of Cho. to 7th verse. — He com-eth a-gain.

4 Rejoice and be glad!
  Now the pardon is free!
  The Just for the unjust
    Hath died on the tree.—*Cho.*

5 Rejoice and be glad!
  For the Lamb, that was slain,
  O'er death is triumphant,
    And liveth again.—*Cho.*

6 Rejoice and be glad!
  For our King is on high;
  He pleadeth for us on
    His throne in the sky.—*Cho.*

7 Rejoice and be glad!
  For He cometh again;
  He cometh in glory,
    The Lamb that was slain.—*Cho.*

28. Revive Us Again.

1 We praise thee, O God! for the Son of Thy love,
  For Jesus, who died, and is now gone above.

Chorus.—Hallelujah! Thine the glory, Hallelujah! Amen.
  Hallelujah! Thine the glory; revive us again.

2 All glory and praise to the Lamb that was slain,
  Who has borne all our sins, and cleansed every stain.—*Cho.*

3 All glory and praise to the God of all grace,
  Who has bought us, and sought us, and guided our ways.—*Cho.*

4 Revive us again; fill each heart with Thy love,
  May each soul be kindled with fire from above.—*Cho.*

Rev. Wm. Paton Mackay, 1866.

29. The Happy Pilgrim.

ANON.

1. I saw a happy pilgrim, In shining garments clad,
His back did bear no burden— He'd laid it at the cross—
Traveling up the mountain, It seemed that he was glad;
The blood of Christ, his Saviour, Had cleans'd him from all dross.

2. The summer sun was shining, But he had found a shield—
His soul was filled with glory As he kept pressing on;
A covert in the desert— Upon life's battle-field;
He heard no other music But what was heaven-born.

REFRAIN.
Then palms of Victory, crowns of Glory, Palms of Victory we shall wear.

3 No pleasure in sin's arbor
  Could catch his eye or ear,
The precious name of Jesus
  Was all he loved to hear.
Thus he kept pressing onward,
  Delighted with the way,
And shouting, Glory! Glory!
  To Jesus all the day.

4 I saw him in the morning,
  On Canaan's sunny plain
Gathering for his Master
  The rich and golden grain;
He bound them up in bundles
  Until the angels come,
To gather in the harvest
  In heaven, his happy home.

5 I saw him in midsummer,
  Still happy on his way,
He'd reached the land of Beulah,
  Where birds sing night and day;
He found a store of honey,
  And wine upon the lees,
And fruit in rich abundance
  Upon life's living trees.

6 I saw him in the evening,
  Life's sun was bending low,
He'd reached the Golden City,—
  His robes still white as snow;
He joined the bridal cortege,
  And drank of the new wine,
And now among the angels
  Eternally doth shine.

30. Is Not This the Land of Beulah?

ANON.   Arranged.

1. I am dwell-ing on the mountain, Where the gold-en sunlight gleams
2. I can see far down the mountain, Where I wandered wea-ry years,
3. I am drink-ing at the fount-ain, Where I ev-er would a-bide;

O'er a land whose wondrous beauty Far ex-ceeds my fond-est dreams;
Oft-en hin-dered in my jour-ney By the ghosts of doubts and fears,
For I've tast-ed life's pure riv-er, And my soul is sat-is-fied;

Where the air is pure, e-the-ral, La-den with the breath of flowers
Brok-en vows and dis-ap-point-ments Thickly sprinkled all the way,
There's no thirst-ing for life's pleas-ures, Nor a-dorn-ing, rich and gay,

Cho.—Is not this the land of Beu-lah, Bless-ed, bless-ed land of light,

D.S. Chorus.

They are bloom-ing by the fountain, 'Neath the am-a-ran-thine bow'rs.
But the Spir-it led, un-er-ring, To the land I hold to-day.
For I've found a rich-er treas-ure, One that fad-eth not a-way.

Where the flow-ers bloom for-ev-er, And the sun is al-ways bright?

4 Tell me not of heavy crosses,
  Nor the burdens hard to bear,
For I've found this great salvation
  Makes each burden light appear;
And I love to follow Jesus,
  Gladly counting all but dross,
Worldly honors all forsaking
  For the glory of the Cross.

5 Oh, the Cross has wondrous glory!
  Oft I've proved this to be true;
When I'm in the way so narrow,
  I can see a pathway through;
And how sweetly Jesus whispers:
  Take the Cross, thou need'st not fear,
For I've tried the way before thee,
  And the glory lingers near.

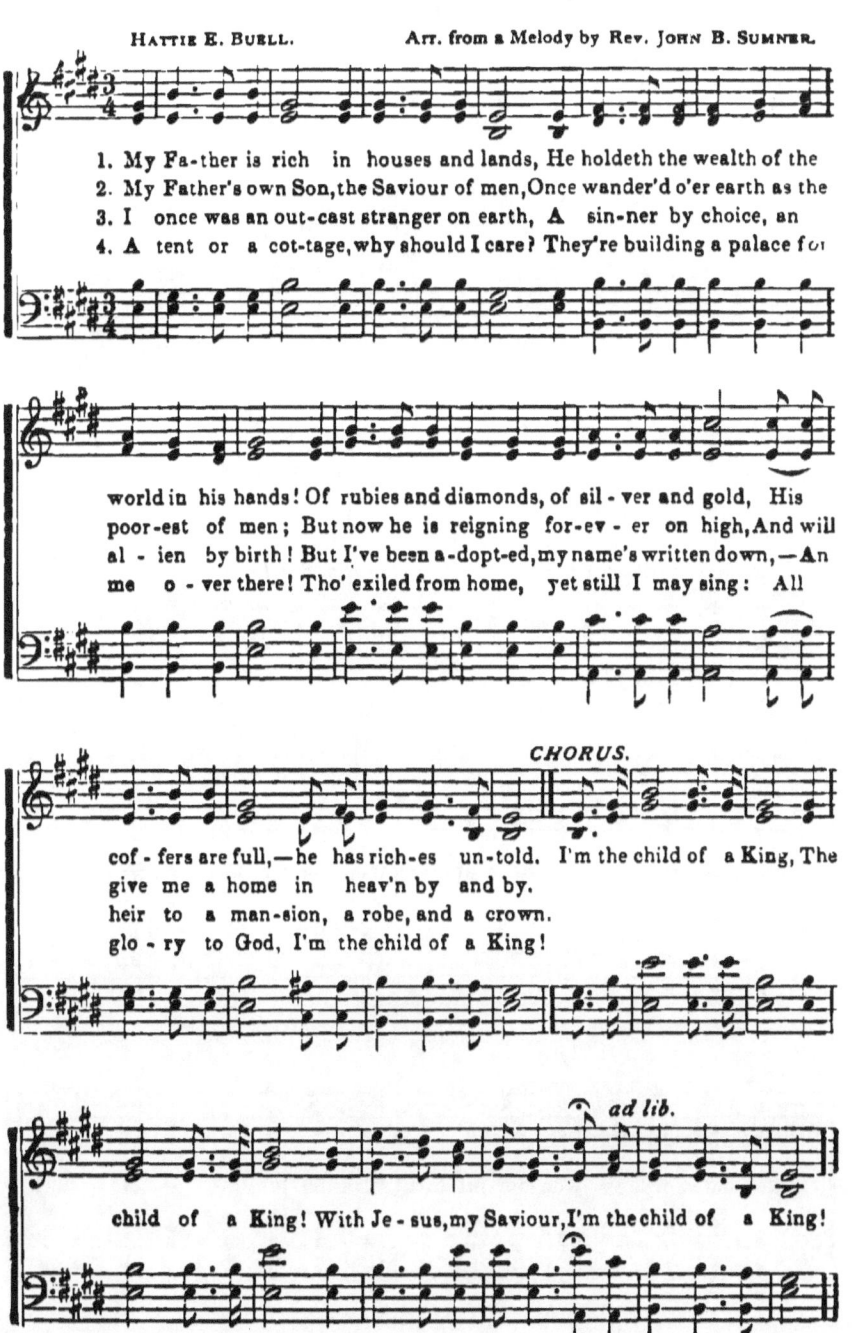

32. Wonderful Love of Jesus.

*"The love of Christ, which passeth knowledge."—*Eph. 3: 19.

E. D. Mund.
E. S. Lorenz.

1. In vain in high and ho-ly lays My soul her grateful voice would raise;
2. A joy by day, a peace by night, In storms a calm, in darkness light;
3. My hope for par-don when I call, My trust for lift-ing when I fall;

For who can sing the worthy praise Of the won-der-ful love of Je - sus?
In pain a balm, in weakness might, Is the won-der-ful love of Je - sus.
In life, in death, my all in all, Is the won-der-ful love of Je - sus.

Chorus.

Won-der - ful love! won-der - ful love! Won-der-ful love of Je - sus!

Won-der - ful love! won-der-ful love! Won-der-ful love of Je - sus!

From "Holy Voices," by per.

33. Redeemed.

FANNY J. CROSBY. WM. J. KIRKPATRICK.

1. Redeemed, how I love to proclaim it, Redeemed by the blood of the Lamb;
2. Redeemed, and so happy in Je-sus, No language my rapture can tell,
3. I think of my blessed Re-deem-er, I think of Him all the day long,
4. I think I shall see in His beau-ty The King in whose law I de-light,
5. I know there's a crown that is waiting In yonder bright mansions for me,

Redeemed thro' His infinite mer-cy, His child and for-ev-er I am.
I know that the light of His presence With me doth continually dwell.
I sing, for I cannot be si-lent, His love is the theme of my song.
Who lov-ing-ly guardeth my footsteps, And giveth me songs in the night.
And soon, with the spirits made perfect, At home with the Lord I shall be.

REFRAIN.

Re-deemed, re-deemed, Redeemed by the blood of the Lamb,
Redeemed, redeemed,

Re-deemed, re-deemed, His child and for-ev-er I am.
Redeemed, redeemed,

Copyright, 1882, by WM. J. KIRKPATRICK. By per.

Lead me gently Home, Father. Concluded.

Lest I fall up-on the way-side, Lead me gent-ly home.
gent-ly home.

---

35. Jesus bids you Come.

W. T. L.   *(May be sung as a Solo.)*   WILL L. THOMPSON.

1. Je - sus bids you come, Je - sus bids you come:
2. Je - sus bids you come, Je - sus bids you come:
3. Je - sus bids you come, Je - sus bids you come:
4. Je - sus bids you come, Je - sus bids you come:

Earn - est - ly for you he's call - ing, Gent - ly at thy
Wea - ry trav - 'ler, do not tar - ry, Je - sus will thy
Voic - es may not al - ways call you, "Late, too late," may
Where 'tis love and joy for - ev - er, Where we'll meet to

heart he's pleading, "Come un - to me, Come un - to me."
bur - dens car - ry, Oh, will you come? Oh, will you come?
yet be - fall you, "Why will ye die?" "Why will ye die?"
part, no, nev - er, Sin - ner, come home, Oh, come, come home.

By permission of W. L. THOMPSON, East Liverpool, O.

36. Bear the Cross for Jesus.

"Take up thy cross and follow me."—MARK 10: 21.

Mrs. ANNIE S. HAWKS. R. LOWRY, by per.

1. Bear the cross for Je-sus, Bear it ev-ery day; Tho' the path be rug-ged, Bear it all the way; Bear the cross for Je-sus, What-so-e'er it be; Bear it, and re-mem-ber All His love for thee.
2. Bear the cross for Je-sus, Bear it thro' the strife, Or in pain and si-lence— What-so-e'er thy life; Bear the cross with pa-tience Tho' you sigh for rest; Just the one He gives you Is for you the best.
3. Bear the cross for Je-sus, Would you know the power Of His grace to save you— Save you hour by hour; Bear the cross for Je-sus, Nev-er mind its weight; We shall leave our bur-den At the gold-en gate.

REFRAIN.

Bear the cross, bear the cross, Bear it ev-ery day; Bear the cross for Je-sus, Bear it all the way.

Copyright, 1876, by REV. R. LOWRY.

38. The Cross.

REV. J. H. STOCKTON. PETER R. BERGEN.

1. The cross! the cross! the blood-stain'd cross! The hallow'd cross I see! Reminding
2. That cross! that cross! that heavy cross, My Saviour bore for me, Which bow'd Him
3. How light! how light! this precious cross, Presented to my view; And while, with
4. The crown! the crown! the glorious crown! The crown of victory! The crown of
5. My tears, un-bid-den, seem to flow For love, unbounded love, Which guides me

CHORUS. *Slow and soft.*

me of precious blood That once was shed for me. Oh, the blood! the precious blood!
to the earth with grief, On sad Mount Cal-va-ry.
care, I take it up, Behold the crown my due.
life! it shall be mine When I shall Jesus see.
thro' this world of woe And points to joys above.

rit.

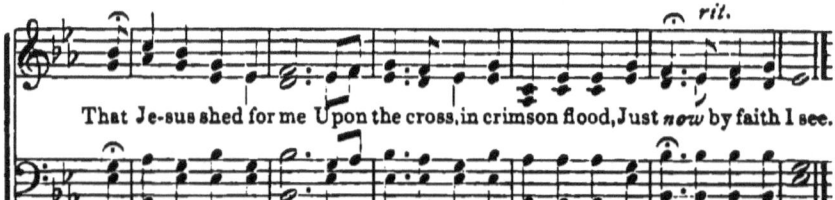

That Jesus shed for me Upon the cross, in crimson flood, Just *now* by faith I see.

39. The Lord will Provide.

PROF. S. C. HARRINGTON.

1. In some way or oth-er the Lord will provide; It may not be *my* way,
2. At some time or oth-er the Lord will provide; It may not be *my* time,
3. Despond then no longer; the Lord will provide; And this be the to-ken—
4. March on, then, right boldly; the sea shall divide; The pathway made glorious,

Used by permission.

The Lord will Provide. Concluded.

It may not be *thy* way, And yet, in His *own* way, "The Lord will provide."
It may not be *thy* time, And yet, in His *own* time, "The Lord will provide."
No word He hath spoken Was ev-er yet broken—"The Lord will provide."
With shoutings victorious, We'll join in the cho-rus, "The Lord will provide."

40. Come to the Saviour.

"Make a joyful noise unto God, all ye lands."—Psa. 66:1.

Geo. F. Root.   Geo. F. Root. By per.

Earnestly.

1. Come to the Sav-iour, make no de-lay; Here in His word He's
2. "Suf-fer the children!" Oh, hear His voice, Let ev-'ry heart leap
3. Think once a-gain, He's with us to-day; Heed now His blest com-

shown us the way; Here in our midst He's standing to-day, Tenderly saying, "Come!"
forth and re-joice, And let us freely make Him our choice; Do not delay, but come.
mands, and obey; Hear now His accents tenderly say, "Will you, my children, come?"

Chorus.

Joy-ful, joy-ful will the meeting be, When from sin our hearts are pure and free,

And we shall gath-er, Sav-iour, with Thee, In our e-ter-nal home.

Used by permission of the John Church Co., owners of the Copyright.

41. I will Shout His Praise in Glory.

P. H. Dingman. Dedicated to H. E. A. Jno. R. Sweney.

1. You ask what makes me happy, my heart so free from care, It is because my
2. I was a friendless wand'rer till Jesus took me in, My life was full of
3. I wish that ev'ry sinner before his throne would bow; He waits to bid them
4. I mean to live for Jesus while here on earth I stay, And when his voice shall

Sav-iour in mercy heard my prayer; He brought me out of darkness and
sor-row, my heart was full of sin; But when the blood so precious spoke
welcome, he longs to bless them now; If they but knew the rapture that
call me to realms of endless day, As one by one we gath-er, re-

now the light I see; O blessed, loving Saviour! to him the praise shall be.
pardon to my soul; Oh, blissful, blissful moment! 'twas joy beyond control.
in his love I see, They'd come and shout salvation, and sing his praise with me.
joicing on the shore, We'll shout his praise in glory, and sing forev-ermore.

CHORUS.

I will shout his praise in glo-ry, So will I, so will I, And we'll all sing halle-lu-jah in heav-en by and by; I will shout his praise in

Copyright, 1888, by Jno. R. Sweney.
From The Joyful Sound, by per. J. J. Hood, Phila., Pa.

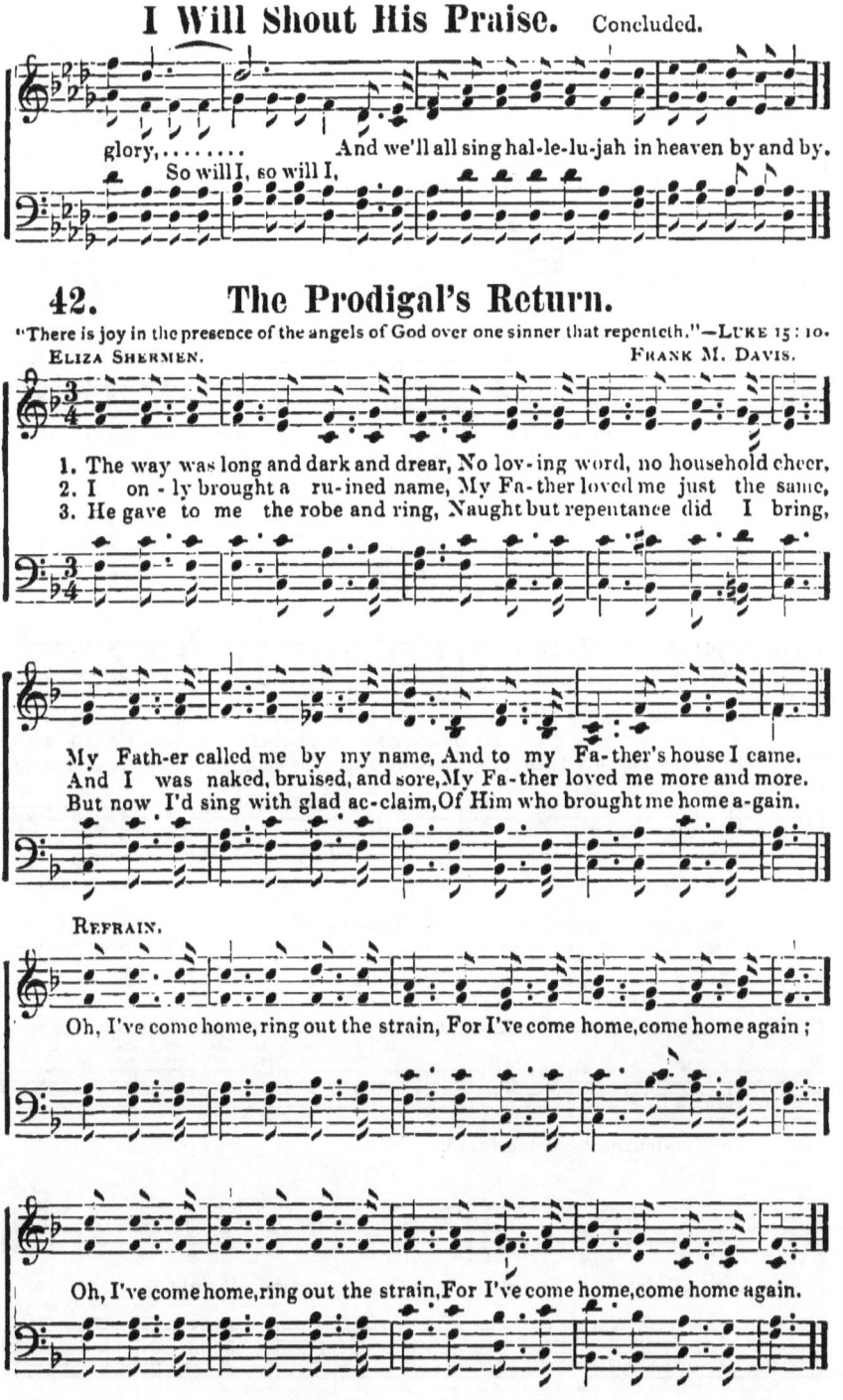

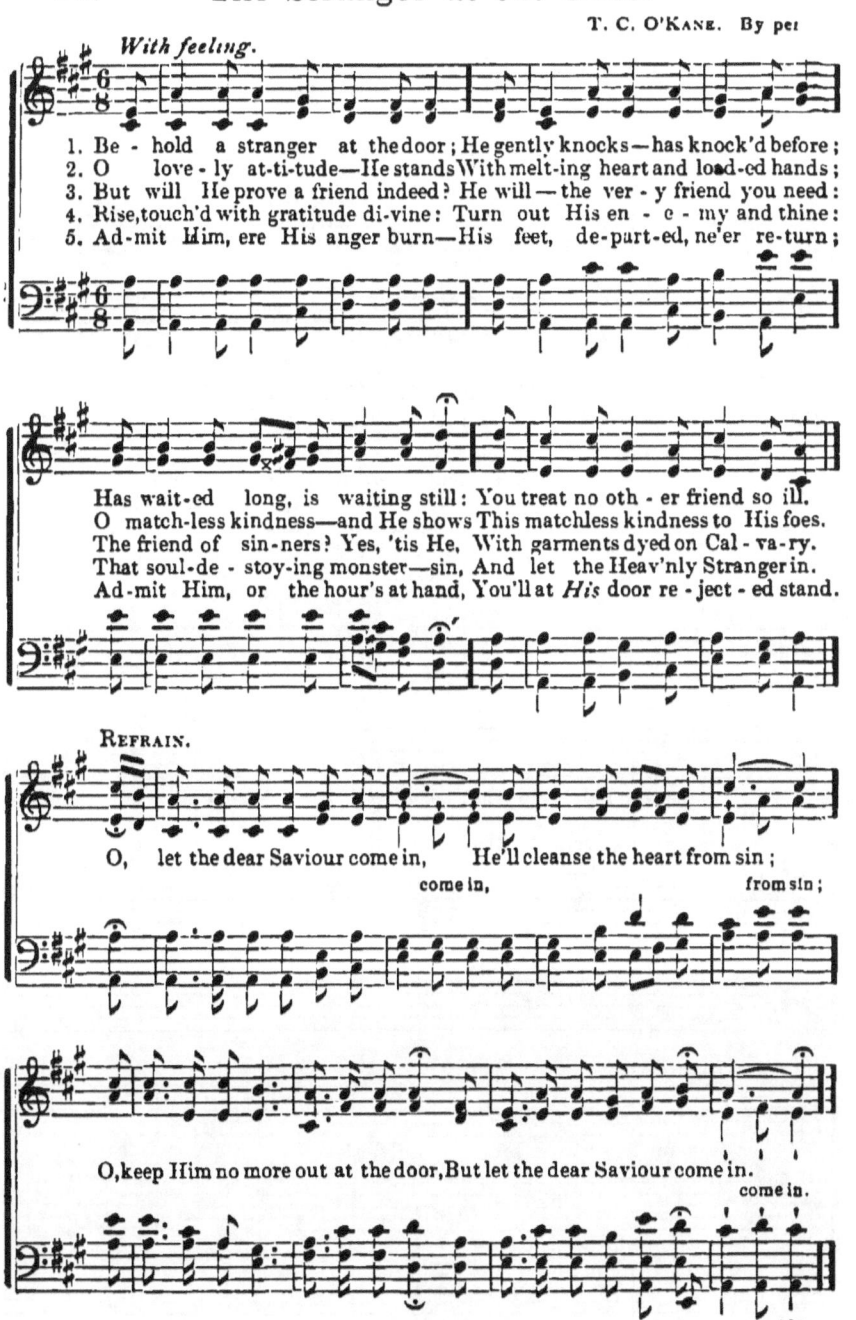

47. The Jericho Service.

F. M. D.
Frank M. Davis. By per.

1. The Great Physician on Jericho's road Is hold-ing a ser-vice to-day,
2. The Great Physician in mercy will heal All those who be-liev-ing will go;
3. The Great Physician is passing this way, Oh, why will you lin-ger and wait?

And multitudes of the poor and the blind Are crowding the great highway.
Their sins tho' red and like scarlet may be, Yet they shall be white as snow.
Be healed to-day, join the sanctified throng, Ere it shall be said, "Too late."

CHORUS.

Are you, my broth-er, among the number Crowding the great highway?

Are you, my broth-er, among the number There to be healed to-day?

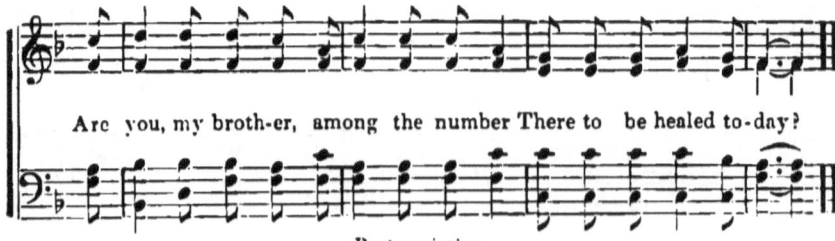

By permission.

51. Safe Within the Vail.

Rev. E. Adams.   J. M. Evans.

1. "Land a-head!" its fruits are waving   O'er the hills of fade-less green;
2. Onward, bark! the cape I'm rounding;   See, the bless-ed wave their hands,
3. There, let go the anchor, rid-ing   On this calm and silvery bay;
4. Now we're safe from all temptation,   All the storms of life are past;

And the liv-ing waters laving Shores where heav'nly forms are seen.
Hear the harps of God resounding From the bright im-mor-tal bands.
Sea-ward fast the tide is gliding, Shores in sunlight stretch a-way.
Praise the Rock of our Sal-va-tion, We are safe at home at last.

CHORUS.

Rocks and storms I'll fear no more, When on that e-ter-nal shore.

Drop the an'-chor! furl the sail! I am safe with-in the vail!

52. Throw Out the Life-Line.

Words and Music by Rev. E. S. UFFORD. From "Converts Praises." 1887, by per.

1. Throw out the Life-Line across the dark wave, There is a broth-er whom some one should save; Somebod-y's broth-er, Oh, who then will dare, To rescue the lost one, his per-il to share?
2. Throw out the Life-Line with hand quick and strong; Why do you tar-ry, my broth-er so long? See! He is sink-ing. Oh, hast-en to-day, Out with the life-boat, away, then away!
3. Throw out the Life-Line to dan-ger-fraught men, Sink-ing in anguish where you've nev-er been; Winds of temp-ta-tion and bil-lows of woe, Will soon hurl them out where the dark waters flow.
4. Soon will this sea-son of res-cue be o'er, Soon will we drift to that fair E-den shore; Then in the dark hour of death may it be, That Jesus will throw out the Life-Line to thee.

CHORUS.

Throw out the Life-Line, Throw out the Life-Line! Some one is drift-ing a-way, Some one is sink-ing to-day.

---

1 This is the Life-line, oh, tempest-tossed men,
Baffled by waves of temptation and sin;
Wild winds of passion, your strength cannot save;
Jesus is mighty, Jesus can save. [brave,

CHORUS.—This is the Life-line,
This is the Life-line,
Jesus can save you to-day;
This is the Life-line,
This is the Life-line,
Jesus can save you to-day.

2 Jesus is able! To you who are driven,
Farther and farther from God and from Heaven;
Helpless and hopeless, overwhelmed by the wave;
We throw out the Life-line, 'tis "Jesus can save."

3 This is the Life-line, oh, grasp it to-day!
See, you are recklessly drifting away;
Voices in warning, shout o'er the wave,
"Grasp the strong Life-line, for Jesus can save."

54. Sowing the Tares.

Dedicated to "Brother Will," M. Cell 1069.

Words by a Convict. M. A. Lee.

Slow. To be sung as a Solo.

1. Sow-ing the tares, when it might have been wheat, Sowing of mal-ice, spite, and de-ceit, We might have sown ro-ses a-mid life's sad cares, While we were so cru-el-ly sow-ing the tares;
2. Sow-ing the tares, how dark the black sin, Mingling a curse with life's sweetest hymn, And heeding no an-guish, no pit-e-ous pray'rs, While we were so cru-el-ly sow-ing the tares;
3. Sow-ing the tares that bring sor-row down, Robs of its jew-els life's fair-est crown; And turning to sil-ver the once golden hairs, Whit-er and whit-er as we sowed the tares;
4. Sow-ing the tares un-der cov-er of night, Which might have been wheat, Grown all golden and bright; O heart, turn to God with repentance and pray'r, And plead for for-give-ness for sow-ing the tares;

REFRAIN.

Sow-ing the tares, Sow-ing the tares, We plead for for-give-ness for sow-ing the tares.

55. He is Just the Same To-day.

"Jesus Christ the same yesterday, and to-day, and forever." —Hebrews xiii: 8.

Mrs. S. Z. KAUFMAN.   I. N. McHOSE.

1. Have you ev-er heard the sto-ry of the babe of Beth-le-hem, Who was worshipped by the an-gels and by wise and ho-ly men, How He taught the learned doc-tors in the Tem-ple far a-way? I am glad to tell you, sin-ners, He is just the same to-day.

2. Have you ev-er heard how Je-sus walk'd up-on the roll-ing sea, To His dear dis-ci-ples toss-ing on the waves of Gal-i-lee, How He res-cues sinking Pe-ter from His dan-ger and dis-may? I am glad to tell you, sin-ners, He is just the same to-day.

3. Once while rest-ing on a pil-low in the ves-sel fast a-sleep There a-rose a might-y tem-pest on the wild and rag-ing deep; "Peace, be still," the Lord commanded, ev-'ry an-gry wave did stay? I am glad to tell you, sin-ners, He is just the same to-day.

4. Sure-ly you have heard how Je-sus prayed, down in Geth-sem-a-ne; How He shed His precious life-blood on the rug-ged, shameful tree, Cru-el thorns His forehead piercing as His spir-it passed a-way; Sin-ner, wont you come and love him? He is just the same to-day.

Copyright, by I. N. McHose. By permission.

He is Just the Same To-day. Concluded.

CHORUS.

He's just the same to-day, Yes, just the same to-day, I'm glad to tell you, sin-ner, He is just the same to-day.

56. Fill Me Now.

Rev. E. H. Stokes, D.D.
Jno. R. Sweney.

1. Hov-er o'er me, Ho-ly Spir-it; Bathe my trembling heart and brow;
2. Thou canst fill me, gracious Spir-it, Tho' I can-not tell Thee how;
3. I am weakness, full of weakness; At Thy sa-cred feet I bow;
4. Cleanse and comfort; bless and save me; Bathe, oh, bathe my heart and brow!

Fill me with Thy hal-low'd presence, Come, oh, come and fill me now.
But I need Thee, great-ly need Thee, Come, oh, come and fill me now.
Blest, di-vine, e-ter-nal Spir-it, Fill with pow'r, and fill me now.
Thou art com-fort-ing and sav-ing, Thou art sweet-ly fill-ing now.

D.S. Fill me with Thy hallow'd presence,—Come, oh, come and fill me now.

CHORUS. *D.S.*

Fill me now, fill me now, Je-sus, come, and fill me now;

Copyright, 1879, by John J. Hood.

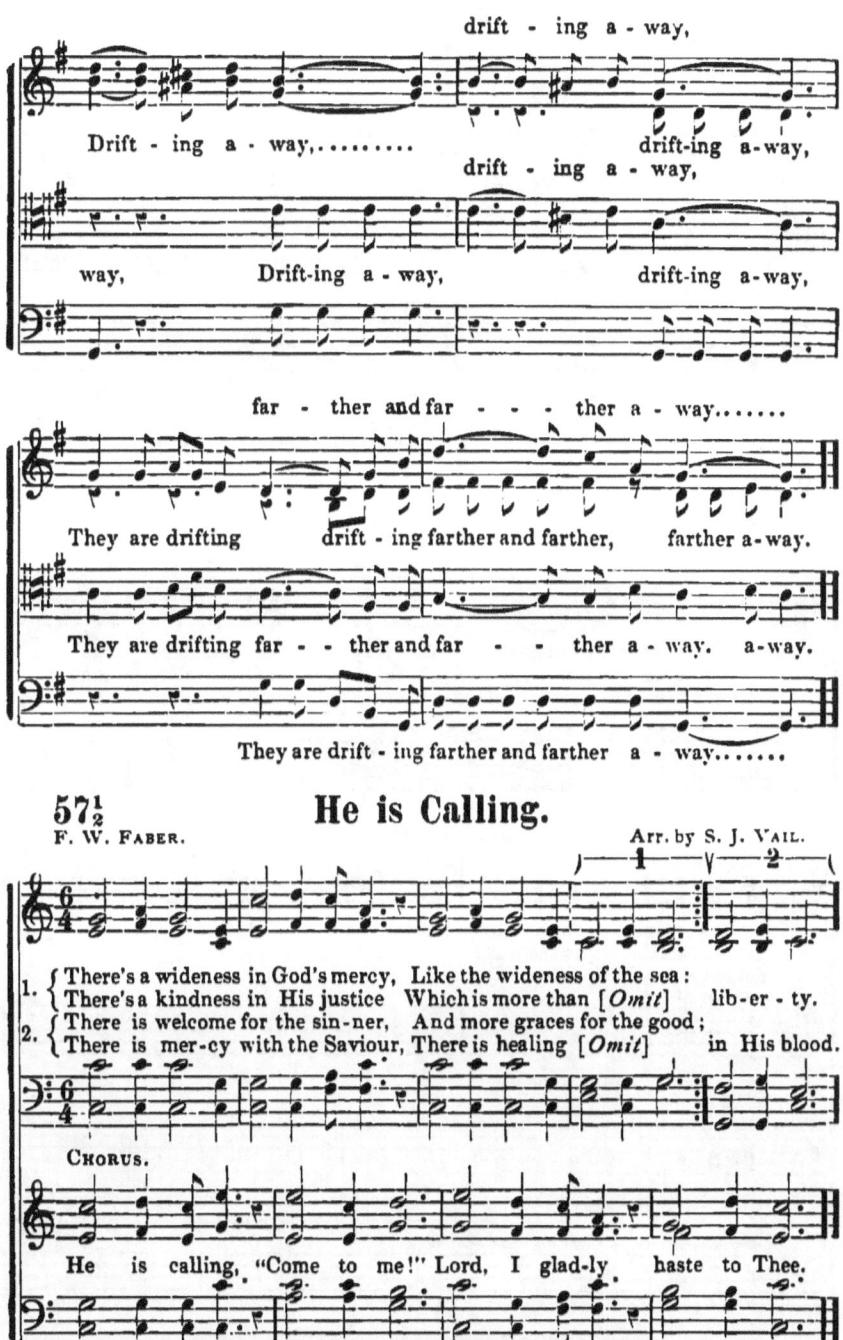

60. I Stood Outside the Gate.

"Enter ye in at the strait gate."—Matt. 7: 13.

Miss Josephine Pollard. Arranged for this Work.

1. I stood outside the gate, A poor wayfaring child; Within my heart there beat A tempest loud and wild; A fear oppressed my soul, That I might be *too late*, And oh, I trembled sore, And pray'd outside the gate.
2. Oh, "mercy!" loud I cried, "Now give me rest from sin!" "I will," a voice replied; And mercy let me in; She bound my bleeding wounds, And sooth'd my heart oppressed; She wash'd a-way my guilt, And gave me peace and rest.
3. In mercy's guise I knew The Saviour long a-bused, Who oft-en sought my heart, And wept when I refused; Oh, what a blest re-turn For all my years of sin! I stood outside the gate, And Je-sus let me in.

CHORUS.

Je-sus is call-ing, is call-ing, is call-ing, Je-sus is call-ing, Ope your heart's door wide, and let Him in.

61. Lead Me, Saviour.

"For thy name's sake lead me, guide me."—PSA. xxx. 3.

F. M. D.
FRANK M. DAVIS.

With espression.

1. Saviour, lead me, lest I stray Gently lead me all the way;
2. Thou the refuge of my soul, When life's stormy billows roll,
3. Saviour, lead me, then at last, When the storm of life is past,

I am safe when by Thy side. I would in Thy love abide.
I am safe when Thou art nigh, All my hopes on Thee rely.
To the land of endless day, Where all tears are wiped away.

CHORUS.

Lead me, lead me, Sav-iour, lead me, lest I stray;

Gent-ly down the stream of time, Lead me, Saviour, all the way.

From "Carols of Joy," by permission.

63. Now I Feel the Sacred Fire.

1. Now I feel the sa-cred fire, Kind-ling, flam-ing, glow-ing,
   High-er still and ris-ing higher, All my soul o'er-flow-ing,
   Life im-mor-tal I re-ceive,—Oh, the won-drous sto-ry!
   I was dead, but now I live, Glo-ry! glo-ry! glo-ry!

2. Now I am from bondage freed, Ev-ery bond is riv-en;
   Je-sus makes me free in-deed, Just as free as heav-en;
   'Tis a glo-rious lib-er-ty— Oh, the won-drous sto-ry!
   I was bound, but now I'm free, Glo-ry! glo-ry! glo-ry!

3 Let the testimony roll,
  Roll through every nation;
  Witnessing from soul to soul,
  This immense salvation,
  Now I know it's full and free;
  Oh, the wondrous story!
  For I feel it saving me,
  Glory! glory! glory!

4 Glory be to God on high,
  Glory be to Jesus!
  He hath brought salvation nigh,
  From all sin He frees us.
  Let the golden harp of God
  Ring the wondrous story;
  Let the pilgrim shout aloud
  Glory! glory! glory!

63½

1 From every stormy wind that blows,
  From every swelling tide of woes,
  There is a calm, a sure retreat:
  'Tis found beneath the mercy-seat.

2 There is a place where Jesus sheds
  The oil of gladness on our heads;
  A place than all besides more sweet:
  It is the blood-bought mercy-seat.

3 Ah! whither could we flee for aid,
  When tempted, desolate, dismayed,
  Or how the hosts of hell defeat,
  Had suffering saints no mercy-seat?

4 There, there on eagle's wings we soar,
  And sin and sense molest no more;
  And heaven comes down our souls to greet,
  While glory crown the mercy-seat.
  —BOEHM.

I'll Feed On Husks No More. Concluded.

Fa-ther's love im-plore, Con-fess my wrong:...... His par-don seek. And feed on husks no more.
His par-don seek,

65 I Stretch My Hands to Thee.

CHAS. WESLEY. Tune—I DO BELIEVE. C. M.

1. Fa-ther, I stretch my hands to Thee, No oth-er help I know;
2. What did Thine on-ly Son en-dure, Be-fore I drew my breath;
CHO.—I do be-lieve, I now be-lieve, That Je-sus died for me,

If Thou withdraw Thy-self from me, Ah, whither shall I go?
What pain, what la-bor to se-cure My soul from end-less death!
And thro' His blood, His pre-cious blood, I shall from sin be free.

3 O Jesus, could I this believe,
  I now should feel Thy power;
  And all my wants Thou wouldst relieve,
  In this accepted hour.

4 Author of faith, to Thee I lift
  My weary, longing eyes;
  O let me now receive that gift!
  My soul without it dies.

70. Mercy is Boundless and Free.

HENRIETTA E. BLAIR. WM. J. KIRKPATRICK. By per.

1. Thanks be to Je-sus, His mer-cy is free; Mer-cy is free,
2. Why on the mountains of sin wilt thou roam? Mer-cy is free,
3. Think of His goodness, His pa-tience and love; Mer-cy is free,
4. Yes, there is par-don for all who be-lieve; Mer-cy is free,

Refrain.—Je-sus, the Sav-iour, is look-ing for thee, look-ing for thee,

mer-cy is free: Sin-ner, that mer-cy is flow-ing for thee,
mer-cy is free: Gent-ly the Spir-it is calling, "Come home,"
mer-cy is free: Pleading thy cause with His Fa-ther a-bove,
mer-cy is free: Come and this mo-ment a blessing re-ceive,

look-ing for thee; Lov-ing-ly, ten-der-ly call-ing for thee,

FINE.

Mer-cy is boundless and free. If thou art will-ing on
Mer-cy is boundless and free. Thou art in darkness O,
Mer-cy is boundless and free. Come and re-pent-ing, O,
Mer-cy is boundless and free. Je-sus is wait-ing. O,

Call-ing and look-ing for thee.

Him to be-lieve, Mer-cy is free, mer-cy is free,
come to the light, Mer-cy is free, mer-cy is free,
give Him thy heart, Mer-cy is free, mer-cy is free.
hear Him pro-claim Mer-cy is free, mer-cy is free.

Copyright, 1882, by W. J. KIRKPATRICK.

Mercy is Boundless and Free. Concluded.

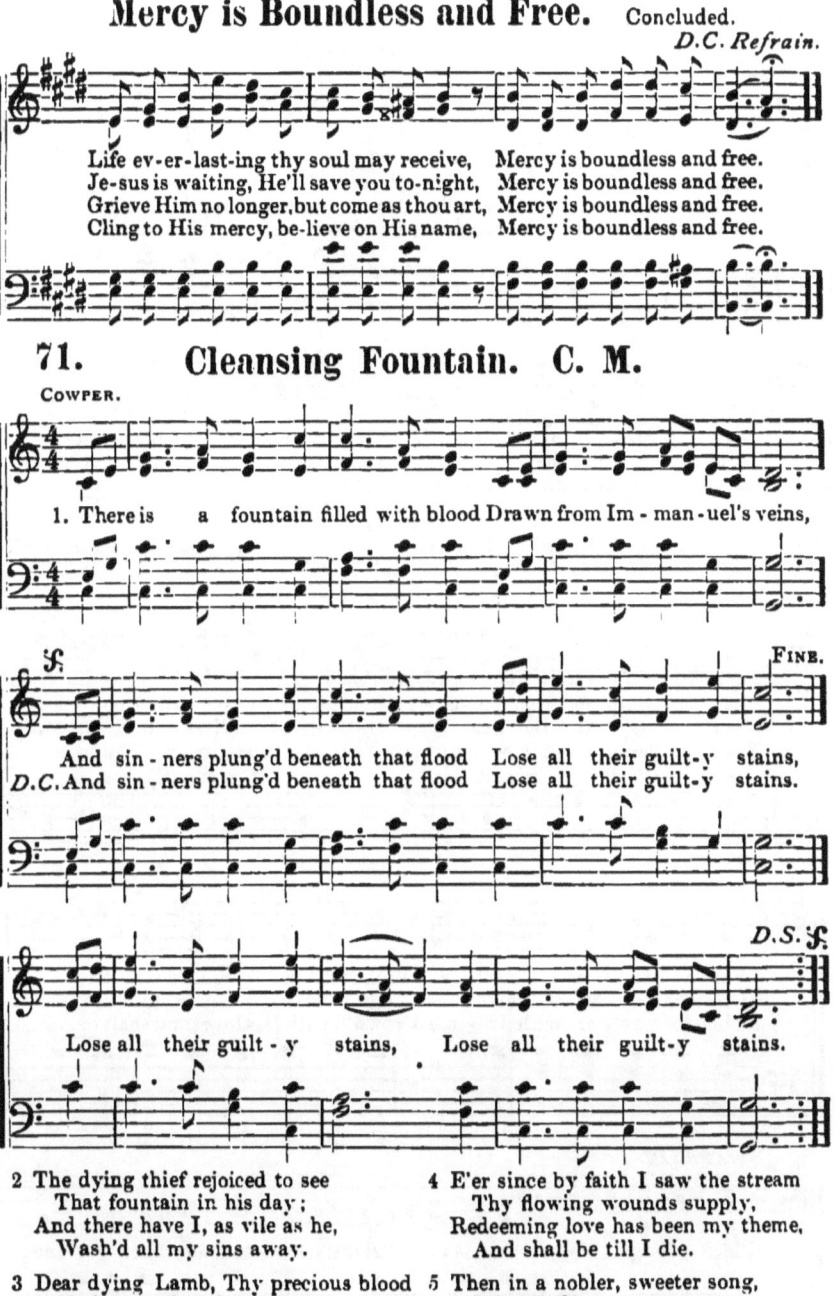

Life ev-er-last-ing thy soul may receive, Mercy is boundless and free.
Je-sus is waiting, He'll save you to-night, Mercy is boundless and free.
Grieve Him no longer, but come as thou art, Mercy is boundless and free.
Cling to His mercy, be-lieve on His name, Mercy is boundless and free.

71. Cleansing Fountain. C. M.
COWPER.

1. There is a fountain filled with blood Drawn from Im-man-uel's veins,
And sin-ners plung'd beneath that flood Lose all their guilt-y stains,
D.C. And sin-ners plung'd beneath that flood Lose all their guilt-y stains.

Lose all their guilt-y stains, Lose all their guilt-y stains.

2 The dying thief rejoiced to see
 That fountain in his day;
 And there have I, as vile as he,
 Wash'd all my sins away.

3 Dear dying Lamb, Thy precious blood
 Shall never lose its power,
 Till all the ransom'd Church of God
 Be saved, to sin no more.

4 E'er since by faith I saw the stream
 Thy flowing wounds supply,
 Redeeming love has been my theme,
 And shall be till I die.

5 Then in a nobler, sweeter song,
 I'll sing Thy power to save,
 When this poor lisping, stam'ring tongue
 Lies silent in the grave.

74. The Glorious Hope.

CHAS. WESLEY.   Arr. by W. J. K.   Tune "Salutation."

1. O glorious hope of perfect love, It lifts me up to things above, It lifts me up to things above, It bears on eagle's wings; It gives my ravished soul a taste, And makes me for some moments feast, And makes me for some

2. Rejoicing now in earnest hope, I stand, and from the mountain-top, I stand, and from the mountain-top See all the land below; Rivers of milk and honey rise, And all the fruits of paradise, And all the

3. A land of corn and wine and oil, Favored with God's peculiar smile, Favored with God's peculiar smile, With every blessing blest; There dwells the Lord our Righteousness, And keeps His own in perfect peace, And keeps His own in

4. Oh, that I might at once go up, No more on this side Jordan stop, No more on this side Jordan stop, But this moment end my legal years, Sorrows and sins, and doubts and fears, Sorrows and sins, and

5. Now, O my Joshua, bring me in! Cast out Thy foes, the inbred sin; Cast out Thy foes, the inbred sin, The carnal mind remove; The purchase of Thy death divide! And oh, with all the sanctified, And oh, with all the

Copyright, 1891, by McDONALD & GILL.

The Glorious Hope. Concluded.

mo - ments   feast   With   Je - sus,   priests and   kings.
par - a - dise   In   end - less   plen - ty   grow.
per - fect   peace   And   ev - er -   last - ing   rest.
doubts and   fears,   A   howl - ing   wil - der -   ness.
sanc - ti - fied,   Give   me   a   lot   of   love.

74½. Step Out on the Promise.

MAGGIE POTTER. Arr. by E. F. M.   E. F. MILLER.

1. O mourn-er in Zi - on, how bless-ed art thou, For Je - sus is
2. O ye that are hun - gry and thirst-y, re-joice! For ye shall be
3. Who sighs for a heart from in - iq - ui - ty free? O, poor troubled
4. Step out on this promise, and Christ thou shalt win, "The blood of His

wait - ing to com-fort thee now, Fear not to re - ly on the
filled; do you hear that sweet voice In - vit - ing you now to the
soul! there's a prom - ise for thee, There's rest, wea-ry one, in the
Son cleanseth us from all sin," It cleans-eth me now, hal - le -

word of thy God; Step out on the prom-ise,—get un-der the blood.
ban-quet of God; Step out on the prom-ise,—get un-der the blood.
bo - som of God; Step out on the prom-ise,—get un-der the blood.
lu - jah to God; I rest on His prom-ise,—I'm un-der the blood.

From "THE SHOUT OF VICTORY." By per.

78. Whiter than Snow.

JAMES NICHOLSON.   WM. G. FISCHER.

1. Lord Jesus, I long to be perfectly whole; I want Thee forever, to live in my soul; Break down ev'ry idol, cast out ev'ry foe; Now wash me, and I shall be whiter than snow.
2. Lord Jesus, look down from Thy throne in the skies, And help me to make a complete sacrifice; I give up myself, and whatever I know, Now wash me, and I shall be whiter than snow.
3. Lord Jesus, for this I most humbly entreat, I wait, blessed Lord, at Thy crucified feet, By faith, for my cleansing, I see Thy blood flow, Now wash me, and I shall be whiter than snow.
4. Lord Jesus, Thou seest I patiently wait, Come now, and within me a new heart create; To those who have sought Thee, Thou never saidst No, Now wash me, and I shall be whiter than snow.

CHORUS.
Whiter than snow, yes, whiter than snow; Now wash me, and I shall be whiter than snow.

By permission.

80. What's the News.

Words arranged by W. H. G.   To Mrs. A. A. A.   Rev. W. H. Geistweit.

1. Whene'er we meet we always say, "What's the news? Pray what's the or-der of the day, What's the news?" His work's re-viv-ing all a-round, And sin-ners hear the gos-pel sound, Re-joic-ing in a Saviour found, That's the news! That's the news!

2. God has pardoned all my sin, That's the news! I feel the wit-ness deep with-in, That's the news! And since he took my sins a-way, And taught me how to watch and pray, I'm hap-py now from day to day, That's the news! That's the news!

3. And now if a-ny one should say, What's the news? O tell him you've be-gun to pray, That's the news! That you have joined the conqu'ring band, And now with joy at God's command, You're marching to the bet-ter land, That's the news! That's the news!

4. Wea-ry pilgrim, hear the call, Bless-ed news! Christ Je-sus came to save us all, That's the news! He died to set poor sin-ners free, That we from death might ran-somed be, And with him reign e-ter-nal-ly, That's the news! That's the news!

Copyright, 1888, by John J. Hood.
From TEMPLE THEMES AND SONGS, by per. J. J. Hood., Phila., Pa.

Roll on the Gospel Chariot. Concluded.

Bells are ring-ing, train is wait-ing, 'Twill soon be out of sight.

Oh, get on the gos-pel char-iot, Yes, get on board to-night,

The bells are ring-ing, train is wait-ing, 'Twill soon be out of sight.

85. Holy Spirit, Faithful Guide.
M. M. WELLS.

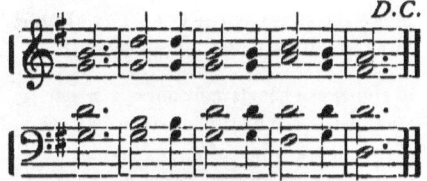

D.C.

2 Ever present, truest Friend,
Ever near, Thine aid to lend,
Leave us not to doubt and fear,
Groping on in darkness drear.
When the storms are raging sore,
Hearts grow faint, and hopes give o'er,
Whisper softly, "Wanderer, come,
Follow me, I'll guide thee home."

1 Holy Spirit, faithful Guide,
Ever near the Christian's side,
Gently lead us by the hand,
Pilgrims in a desert land.
Weary souls, fore'er rejoice,
While they hear that sweetest voice
Whispering softly, "Wanderer, come,
Follow me, I'll guide thee home."

3 When our days of toil shall cease,
Waiting still for sweet release,
Nothing left but heaven and prayer,
Wondering if our names are there;
Wading deep the dismal flood,
Pleading naught but Jesus' blood;
Whisper softly, "Wanderer, come,
Follow me, I'll guide thee home."

86. At Even, Ere the Sun was Set.

SESSIONS. L. M. LUTHER ORLANDO EMERSON.

1. At e-ven, ere the sun was set, The sick, O Lord, around Thee lay;
2. Once more 'tis e-ven-tide; and we, Oppress'd with various ills, draw near;
3. O Saviour Christ, our woes dispel; For some are sick, and some are sad,
4. And all, O Lord, crave perfect rest, And to be whol-ly free from sin,
5. Thy touch has still its ancient power, No word from Thee can fruitless fall;

Oh, in what divers pains they met! Oh, with what joy they went a-way!
What if Thy form we cannot see? We know and feel that Thou art here.
And some have never loved Thee well, And some have lost the love they had.
And they who fain would serve Thee best Are conscious most of sin within.
Hear, in this sol-emn evening hour, Lord, in Thy mer - cy heal us all.

---

1 I thirst, Thou wounded Lamb of God,
To wash me in Thy cleansing blood;
To dwell within Thy wounds; then pain
Is sweet, and life or death is gain.

2 Take my poor heart, and let it be
Forever closed to all but Thee:
Seal Thou my breast, and let me wear
That pledge of love forever there.

3 How blest are they who still abide
Close sheltered in Thy bleeding side!
Who thence their life and strength derive,
And by Thee move, and in Thee live.

4 What are our works but sin and death
Till Thou Thy quickening Spirit breathe?
Thou giv'st the power Thy grace to move;
O wondrous grace! O boundless love!

5 How can it be, Thou heavenly King,
That Thou shouldst us to glory bring?
Make slaves the partners of Thy throne,
Decked with a never-fading crown?

6 Hence our hearts melt, our eyes o'erflow,
Our words are lost, nor will we know,
Nor will we think of aught beside,
"My Lord, my Love is crucified."

NICOLAUS L. ZINZENDORF. Tr. by J. WESLEY.

---

1 Praise God, from whom all blessings flow!
Praise Him, all creatures here below!
Praise Him above, ye heavenly host!
Praise Father, Son, and Holy Ghost!

2 Eternal are Thy mercies, Lord!
Eternal truth attends Thy word,
Thy praise shall sound from shore to shore,
Till suns shall rise and set no more.

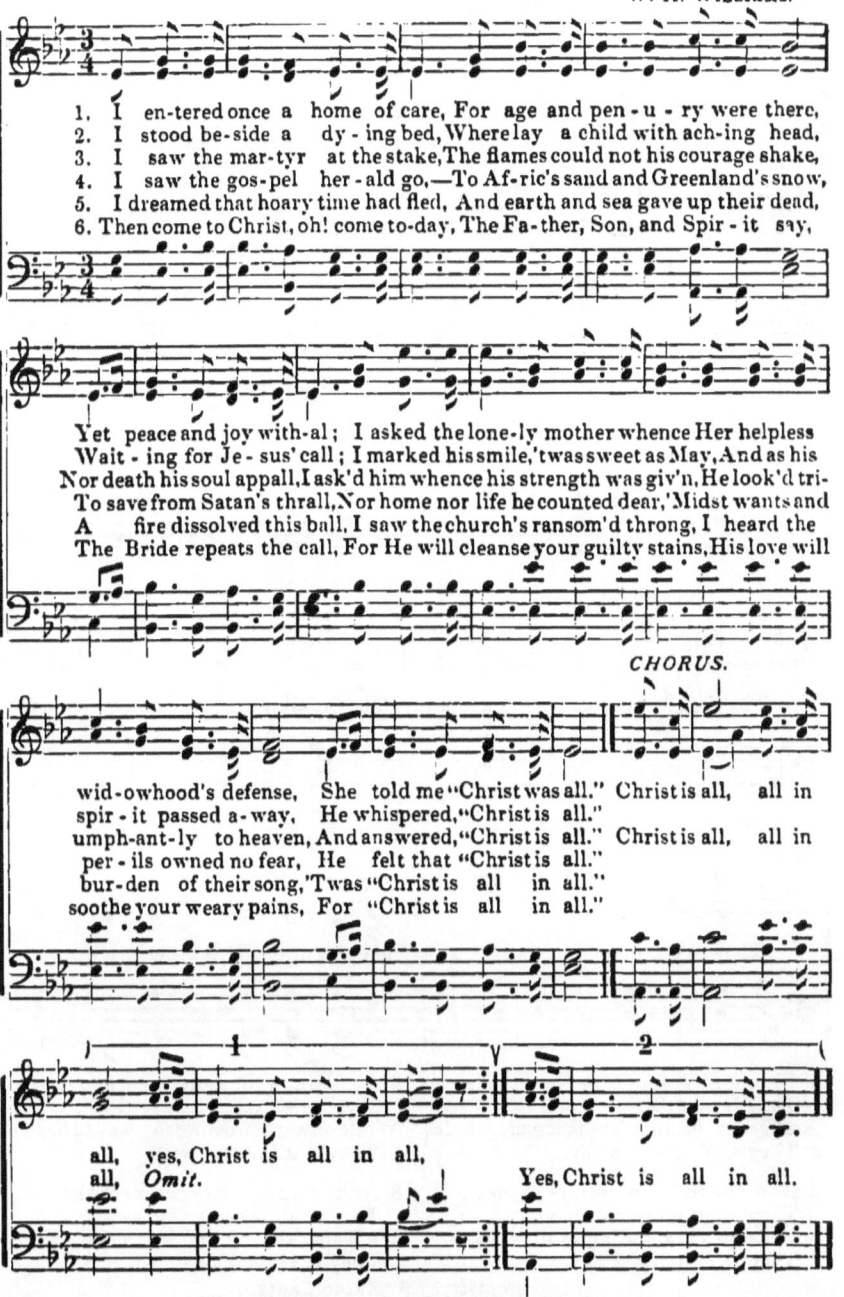

88. All Taken Away.

R. KELSO CARTER, (*except first verse*). A. A.

1. Did you hear what Jesus said to me? "They're all taken a-way, away,"
2. Oh, this wondrous grace so free and full; They're all taken a-way, away,
3. Now the cleansing streams of mercy flow; They're all taken a-way, away,
4. I have plung'd beneath the crimson tide; They're all taken a-way, away,

My sins are pardoned and I am free, They're all tak-en a-way.
Tho' red like crimson, they're now as wool; They're all tak-en a-way.
My sins like scarlet are white as snow; They're all tak-en a-way.
And now by faith I am pu-ri-fied; They're all tak-en a-way.

CHORUS.

They're all tak-en a-way, away, They're all tak-en a-way, a-way,
They're all tak-en away, away, My sins are all tak-en a-way.

5 Oh, the cleansing blood has washed my
   They're all taken away, away; [soul;
And Jesus' healing has made me whole;
   They're all taken away.

6 Now the Spirit witnesses to me;
   They're all taken away, away;
And keeps me standing in liberty;
   They're all taken away.

7 So I praise the Lord for sins forgiven,
   They're all taken away, away;
While onward pressing my way to heav'n;
   They're all taken away.

8 And when in glory we meet above;
   They're all taken away, away;
We'll sing the song of Redeeming Love;
   They're all taken away.

Copyright, 1891, by R. KELSO CARTER.

90. The Song of Jubilee.

MRS. HARRIET E. JONES. Or Air—Marching through Georgia. FRANK M. DAVIS.

1. Sing the Christian's marching song, and sing it with a will, Let the mu - sic
2. How the soldiers shouted when they heard the dear old song! How their faces
3. Yes, and there were loyal men, whose hearts with joy did swell, As they bore the
4. Let us sing the dear old song, and sing it o'er and o'er, Sing it with the

float along o'er val-ley, plain and hill; Sing as did the saints of old—in
brightened as the mu - sic roll'd a-long! How that song of Je-sus helped to
flag along of Him they loved so well; Blood-stained flag of One who died that
spir - it of the dear saint's gone before; Sing it thro' our marchings here, then

heaven singing still. While they were marching to glory. O sing, O sing the
make the feeble strong, While they were marching to glory.
they with Him might dwell. While they were marching to glory.
sing it ev-er-more, While we are marching to glo-ry.

CHORUS.

song of ju-bi-lee, O sing, O sing of Him who set you free, Sing of Him each
step you take while marching to the sea, While you are marching to glo - ry.

Copyright, 1893, by H. H. HADLEY.

91. Rest and Home.

Mrs. Harriet E. Jones. S. C. Foster.

1. Way down upon the paths forbidden, Once I did roam;
   Far from the blessed Saviour hidden, Far from sweet rest and home:
   Oh! 'twas a pathway dark and lonely, Till one sweet day,
   When I had learned that Jesus only, Washed all my sins away.

CHORUS.
Glory, glory hallelujah! I no longer roam;
Now I am happy in my Saviour, I have found sweet rest and home.

2 Saved, from the depths of degradation,
  Sins' dread abyss,
  Praise God, there's now no condemna-
   As Jesus owns me His;   [tion,
  Since all my sins the blood doth cover,
  Sweet peace is mine;
  Now, I can sing the story over—
  Sing, of the love divine.

3 Oh! I am drinking from the fountain
  So deep and wide;
  Up to the heights of grace I'm mounting
  Close by my Saviour's side.
  Come, brothers, from the byways dreary,
  No longer roam;
  Lo! Jesus calls in language cheery;
  "Come, find in Me sweet home."

Copyright, 1894, by R. Kelso Carter.

I Know Thou Art Praying For Me. Concluded.

93½ Sweetly Resting.

Dedicated to Chaplain C. C. McCabe.

MARY D. JAMES. W. WARREN BENTLEY. By per.

1. In the rift-ed Rock I'm rest-ing, Safe-ly shel-ter'd, I a-bide;
2. Long pur-sued by sin and Sa-tan, Wea-ry, sad, I long'd for rest;
3. Peace, which passeth un-der-stand-ing, Joy, the world can nev-er give,
4. In the rift-ed Rock I'll hide me, Till the storms of life are past,

There no foes nor storms mo-lest me, While with-in the cleft I hide.
Then I found this heav'n-ly shel-ter, O-pened in my Savior's breast.
Now in Je-sus I am find-ing; In His smiles of love I live.
All se-cure in this blest ref-uge, Heed-ing not the fierc-est blast.

REFRAIN.

Now I'm rest-ing, Sweetly rest-ing, In the cleft once made for me:

Je-sus, bless-ed Rock of A-ges, I will hide my-self in Thee.

97.
CHARLES WESLEY.

Lenox. H. M.

LEWIS EDSON.

1. Blow ye the trumpet, blow, The gladly-solemn sound! Let all the nations know,
2. Jesus, our great High Priest, Hath full atonement made, Ye weary spirits, rest;

To earth's re - mot - est bound, The year of ju - bi - lee is come!
Ye mournful souls, be glad: The year of ju - bi - lee is come!

The year of ju - bi - lee is come! Return, ye ransomed sin-ners, home
The year of ju - bi - lee is come! Return, ye ransomed sin-ners, home.

3 Extol the Lamb of God,
 The all-atoning Lamb;
 Redemption in His blood
 Throughout the world proclaim:
The year of jubilee is come!
Return, ye ransomed sinners, home.

4 Ye slaves of sin and hell,
 Your liberty receive,
 And safe in Jesus dwell.
 And blest in Jesus live:
The year of jubilee is come!
Return, ye ransomed sinners, home.

5 Ye who have sold for naught
 Your heritage above,
 Shall have it back unbought,
 The gift of Jesus' love:
The year of jubilee is come!
Return, ye ransomed sinners, home

6 The gospel trumpet hear,
 The news of heavenly grace;
 And, saved from earth, appear
 Before your Saviour's face:
The year of jubilee is come!
Return, ye ransomed sinners, home.

---

1 Arise, my soul, arise;
 Shake off thy guilty fears;
 The bleeding Sacrifice
 In my behalf appears;
Before the throne my Surety stands,
My name is written on His hands.

2 He ever lives above,
 For me to intercede;
 His all-redeeming love,
 His precious blood to plead;
His blood atoned for all our race,
And sprinkles now the throne of grace.

3 Five bleeding wounds He bears,
 Received on Calvary;
 They pour effectual prayers,
 They strongly plead for me:
"Forgive him, O forgive," they cry,
"Nor let that ransomed sinner die."

4 The Father hears Him pray,
 His dear annointed One:
 He cannot turn away
 The presence of His Son:
His Spirit answers to the blood,
And tells me I am born of God.

5 My God is reconciled;
 His pardoning voice I hear;
 He owns me for His child;
 I can no longer fear:
With confidence I now draw nigh.
And, "Father, Abba, Father," cry.

CHARLES WESLEY

99. I'm Believing and Receiving.

"Believing, ye rejoice with joy unspeakable."—1 Pet. 1:8.

H. H. B.   COMMANDANT HERBERT BOOTH. By per.

1. Sins of years are wash'd a-way, Blackest stains be-come as snow,
2. Doubts and fears are borne a-long On the cur-rent's ceaseless flow,
3. Ease and wealth become as dross, Worthless, earth's delight and show,
4. Self-ish-ness is lost in love, Love for Him whose love you know,
5. Fight-ing is a great de-light, Nev-er will you fear the foe,

Dark-est night is changed to day, When you to the riv-er go.
Sor-row changes in-to song, When you to the riv-er go.
All your boast is in the cross, When you to the riv-er go.
All your treas-ure is a-bove, When you to the riv-er go.
Armed by King Je-ho-vah's might, When you to the riv-er go.

mf CHORUS.

I'm be-liev-ing and re-ceiv-ing, While I to the riv-er go.

And my heart its waves are cleansing Whit-er than the driv-en snow.

I'll Bear It, Lord, For Thee. Concluded.

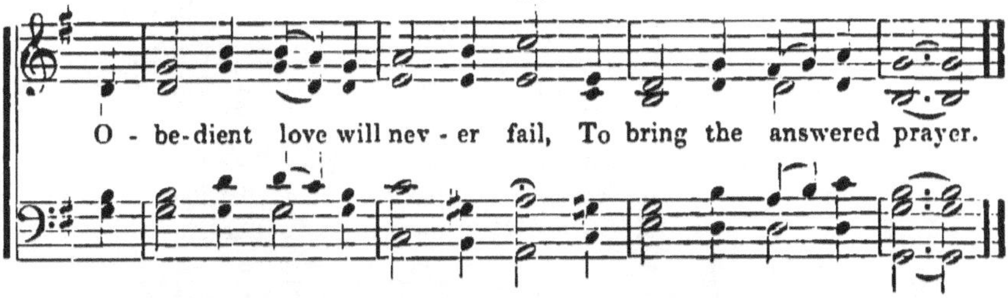

O - be-dient love will nev - er fail, To bring the answered prayer.

101. We'll Never Say Good By.

"We shall never say 'good by' in heaven."—The words of a dying Christian woman.

Mrs. E. W. CHAPMAN. J. H. TENNEY.

1. Our friends on earth we meet with pleasure, While swift the moments fly,
2. How joy - ful is the tho't that lin-gers, When loved ones cross death's sea,
3. No part - ing words shall e'er be spok-en In that bright land of flowers,

Yet ev - er comes the tho't of sadness That we must say good by.
That when our la-bors here are end-ed, With them we'll ev - er be.
But songs of joy, and peace, and gladness, Shall ev - er - more be ours.

CHORUS.

We'll nev-er say good by in heaven, We'll nev-er say good by,......

Repeat Chorus pp

For in that land of joy and song, We'll nev-er say good by.

Copyright, 1889, by JOHN J. HOOD. By permission.

102. Give Me a Heart Like Thine.

JOSHUA GILL.

1. Give me a heart like Thine, Give me a heart like Thine; By Thy wonderful pow-er, By Thy grace ev-ery hour: Give me a heart like Thine.
2. Help me to live like Thee, Help me to live like Thee; By Thy wonderful pow-er, By Thy grace ev-ery hour: Help me to live like Thee.
3. Help me to love like Thee, Help me to love like Thee; By Thy wonderful pow-er, By Thy grace ev-ery hour: Help me to love like Thee.

4 Help me to pray like Thee.
5 Help me to give like Thee.
6 Help me to speak like Thee.
7 Help me to work like Thee.

Copyright, 1888, by JOSHUA GILL.

103. I am Bound for the Kingdom.

1. { Whith-er goest thou, pilgrim stranger, Wand'ring thro' this gloomy vale? }
   { Know'st thou not 'tis full of danger, And will not thy courage fail? }
2. { Pil - grim thou hast justly called me, Pass-ing thro' the waste so wide, }
   { But no harm will e'er be-fall me While I'm blest with such a guide. }

REFRAIN.

I am bound for the kingdom, Will you go to glory with me? Hallelujah, Praise ye the Lord!

3 Such a guide? no guide attends thee,
  Hence for thee my fears arise:
  If some guardian power befriend thee,
  'Tis unseen by mortal eyes.

4 Yes, unseen, but still believe me,
  Such a guide my steps attend;
  He'll in every strait relieve me,
  He will guide me to the end.

5 Pilgrim, see that stream before thee,
  Darkly winding through the vale;
  Should its deadly waves roll o'er thee
  Would not then thy courage fail?

6 No, that stream has nothing frightful,
  To its brink my steps I'll bend,
  Thence to plunge 'twill be delightful
  There my pilgrimage will end.

104. All for Sinners.

Mrs. Harriet E. Jones. — Frank M. Davis.

1. In the gar-den prostrate ly-ing, Thro' long hours of ag-o-ny;
   Un-to God the Son is crying; "Grant this cup may pass from me."
2. Je-sus pleads till blood-drops gather, Till the vic-to-ry is won;
   Sweetly say-ing, "O my Fa-ther, Not my will but Thine be done."
3. Hark! the mul-ti-tude are cry-ing, As our Lord is led a-way;
   "Cru-ci-fy Him! cru-ci-fy Him! Save Bar-ab-bas, Je-sus slay."
4. Up the hill-side steep and drear-y, All a-long the rug-ged road;
   Per-se-cu-ted, faint and wea-ry, Je-sus bears the dreadful load.

CHORUS.
All for sinners, all for sinners, All the bit-ter ag-o-ny;
All for sinners, all for sinners, Cal-va-ry, Geth-sem-a-ne.

5 To the cross they nail our Saviour,
Spit upon Him, mock, deride;
From His side the blood so precious,
Flows for us a healing tide.

6 Hark, O sinner! "it is finished,"
Rocks are rent while Jesus cries,
"It is finished, it is finished,"
Bows His sacred head and dies.

Copyright. 1893, by H. H. Hadley.

108. Realms of Beauty.

Words arranged by N. L. H.   Music arranged by Prof. O. S. SCHNAUFFER.
Dedicated to Rev. N. L. Hoopingarner.

1. From this world of sin and sor-row, We are pass-ing one by one; But there will be a bright to-morrow, It is bet-ter farther on.
2. Ma-ny loved ones have de-part-ed To their glo-rious home a-bove; And while we mourn we'll be light-hearted, For they're resting in His love.

CHORUS.
Far-ther on in the line of du-ty, Far a-way on the golden shore;
We shall rest in the realms of beau-ty, When the toil of life is o'er.

3 We have heard them tell the story,
   Of their precious Saviour's love;
And while they spake a beam of glory,
   Rested on them from above.

4 Many are down in the valley,
   And can hear the waters roar;
But still they trust their blessed Saviour,
   Who will bear them safely o'er.

5 And with angels bright and lovely,
   Robed in garments pure and white;
There they will sing and shout forever,
   In the home of saints in light.

6 Soon we all will be called over,
   And shall meet each other there;
To live in joy with God forever,
   Free from sorrow, toil and care.

109. In Evil Long I Took Delight.

Rev. WM. HENRY HAVERGAL.

1. In e-vil long I took de-light, Un-awed by shame or fear,
2. I saw One hang-ing on a tree, In ag-o-nies and blood,
3. Sure nev-er till my lat-est breath Can I for-get that look:
4. A sec-ond look He gave, which said, "I free-ly all for-give;
5. Thus, while His death my sin dis-plays In all its blackest hue,

Till a new ob-ject struck my sight, And stopped my wild ca-reer.
Who fixed His lan-guid eyes on me, As near His cross I stood.
It seemed to charge me with His death, Tho' not a word He spoke.
This blood is for thy ran-som paid; I die that thou mayst live."
Such is the mys-te-ry of grace, It seals my par-don too.

---

110. Bartimeus.

ROBERT ROBINSON.

1. Come, Thou Fount of ev-ery blessing, Tune my heart to sing Thy grace;
2. Teach me some me-lo-dious son-net, Sung by flam-ing tongues a-bove;
3. Je-sus sought me when a stranger, Wandering from the fold of God;
4. O to grace how great a debt-or Dai-ly I'm constrained to be!
5. Prone to wan-der, Lord, I feel it, Prone to leave the God I love;

Streams of mer-cy nev-er ceasing, Call for songs of loud-est praise.
Praise the mount—I'm fixed upon it— Mount of Thy re-deem-ing love!
He, to res-cue me from danger, In-ter-posed His precious blood.
Let Thy goodness, like a fet-ter, Bind my wandering heart to Thee:
Here's my heart, O take and seal it; Seal it for Thy courts a-bove.

113. He Saves the Drunkard Too.

HENRY H. HADLEY.   GEORGE KINSLEY.

1. My Saviour can the drunkard save, For He has res - cued me.
2. He once the kneeling lep - er cleans'd, And gave him life a - new;
3. While waiting at Be - thes-da's pool He made the lame to walk;
4. Then standing by the widow's son, Our pity-ing Lord we view.

One thing I know: I once was blind, But now, thank God, I see.
He res-cued Pe - ter from the wave; He saves the drunk-ard too.
The beg-gar healed at Jer - i - cho, And caus'd the dumb to talk.
He sav'd poor Ma - ry Mag - da - lene; He saves the drunk-ard too.

5 The withered hand His voice restored,
   And He the damsel raised.
   Called Lazarus forth, and they who saw
   Stood wondering and amazed.

6 Oh, weary sinner, come to Him,
   'Tis all that thou canst do.
   Remember, He alone can keep
   And save the drunkard too.

Copyright, 1890, by WM. J. KIRKPATRICK.

---

1 How vain are all things here below!
   How false, and yet how fair!
   Each pleasure hath its poison too,
   And every sweet a snare.

2 The brightest things below the sky
   Give but a flattering light;
   We should suspect some danger nigh,
   Where we possess delight.

3 The fondness of a creature's love,—
   How strong it strikes the sense!
   Thither the warm affections move,
   Nor can we call them thence.

4 My Saviour, let Thy beauties be
   My soul's eternal food;
   And grace command my heart away
   From all created good.

ISAAC WATTS.

115. The Old Time Religion.

For "Rescue Songs."
Arr. by Grant C. Tuller.

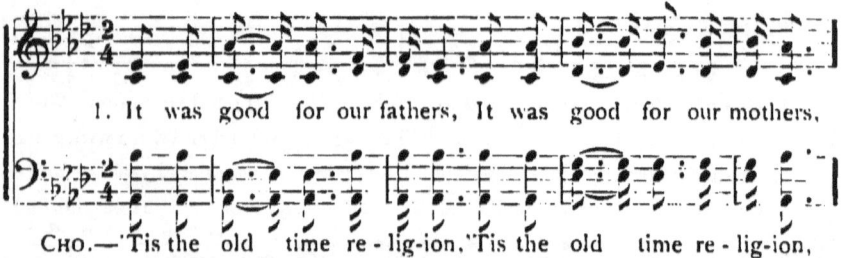

1. It was good for our fathers, It was good for our mothers,

Cho.—'Tis the old time re-lig-ion, 'Tis the old time re-lig-ion,

For our sisters and our brothers, And 'tis good enough for me.

'Tis the old time re-lig-ion, And 'tis good enough for me.

2 :||: Makes me love everybody, :||:
And 'tis good enough for me.

3 :||: It was good for the Prophet Daniel, :||:
And 'tis good enough for me.

4 :||: It was good for the Hebrew children, :||:
And 'tis good enough for me.

5 :||: It was good for Paul and Silas, :||:
And 'tis good enough for me.

6 :||: It will save a poor lost sinner, :||:
And 'tis good enough for me.

7 :||: It will lighten every burden, :||:
And 'tis good enough for me.

8 :||: It will make you leave off drinking, :||:
And 'tis good enough for me.

9 :||: It brought me out of bondage, :||:
And 'tis good enough for me

10 :||: It will sanctify you wholly, :||:
And 'tis good enough for me.

11 :||: It will do when you are dying, :||:
And 'tis good enough for me.

12 :||: It will take us home to heaven, :||:
And 'tis good enough for me.

Copyright, 1894, by Grant C. Tuller.

116. On the Cross of Calvary.

1. On the Cross of Cal-va-ry, Je-sus died for you and me; There He shed His precious blood, That from sin we might be free. Oh, the cleansing stream does flow, And it washes white as snow: It was for me that Jesus died On the Cross of Cal-va-ry.
2. Oh, what wondrous, wondrous love, Bro't me down at Jesus' feet; Oh, such won-drous, dying love, Asks a sac-ri-fice complete. Here I give myself to Thee, Soul and body Thine to be: It was for me Thy blood was shed On the Cross of Cal-va-ry.
3. Take me, Je-sus, I am Thine, Wholly Thine, for-ev-er-more; Bless-ed Je-sus, Thou art mine, Dwell within, forevermore. Cleanse, oh, cleanse my heart from sin, Make and keep me pure within: It was for this Thy blood was shed On the Cross of Cal-va-ry.
4. Clouds and darkness veil'd the skies, When the Lord was cru-ci-fied; "It is finish'd!" was His cry, When He bow'd His head and died. It is finish'd, it is finish'd, All the world may now go free: It was for me that Jesus died On the Cross of Cal-va-ry.

CHORUS.
Of Cal-va-ry,.......... Of Cal-va-ry,..........
Of Cal-va-ry, Of Cal-va-ry,
It was for me that Je-sus died On the Cross of Cal-va-ry.

118. I'm Kneeling at the Mercy-seat.

(Use any Common Metre Hymn with this Chorus.)

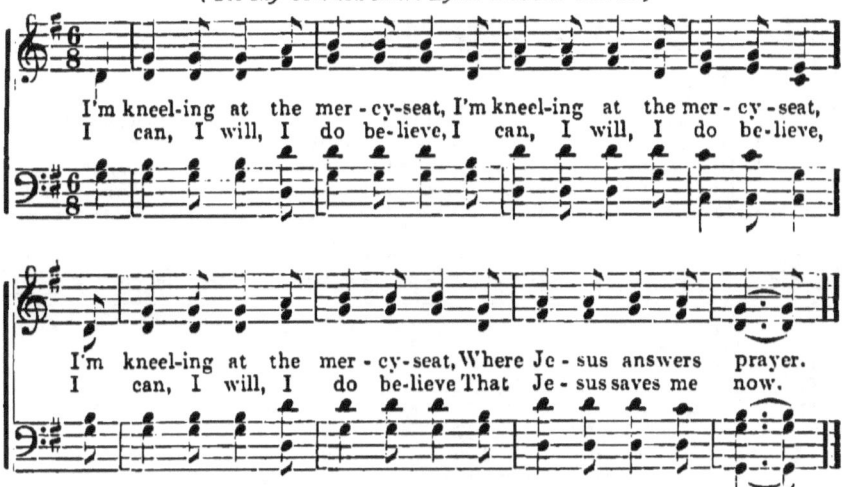

I'm kneel-ing at the mer-cy-seat, I'm kneel-ing at the mer-cy-seat,
I can, I will, I do be-lieve, I can, I will, I do be-lieve,

I'm kneel-ing at the mer-cy-seat, Where Je-sus answers prayer.
I can, I will, I do be-lieve That Je-sus saves me now.

1 Jesus, Thine all-victorious love
  Shed in my heart abroad;
  Then shall my feet no longer rove,
  Rooted and fixed in God.

2 O that in me the sacred fire
  Might now begin to glow;
  Burn up the dross of base desire,
  And make the mountains flow.

3 O that it now from heaven might fall,
  And all my sins consume;
  Come, Holy Ghost, for Thee I call;
  Spirit of burning, come.

4 Refining fire, go through my heart;
  Illuminate my soul:
  Scatter Thy life through every part,
  And sanctify the whole.

119. Blest be the Tie that Binds.

JOHN FAWCETT.   Tune, DENNIS. S. M.

1. Blest be the tie that binds Our hearts in Chris-tian love;
2. Be-fore our Fa-ther's throne We pour our ar-dent pray'rs;
3. We share our mu-tual woes, Our mu-tual bur-dens bear;

The fel-low-ship of kin-dred minds Is like to that a-bove.
Our fears, our hopes, our aims are one, Our com-forts and our cares.
And oft-en for each oth-er flows The sym-pa-thiz-ing tear.

120. Jesus for Me.

W. J. K.
WM. J. KIRKPATRICK, by per.

1. Je - sus, my Saviour, is all things to me, Oh, what a won - der - ful
2. Je - sus in sickness, and Je - sus in health, Je - sus in pov - er - ty,
3. He is my Ref - uge, my Rock, and my Tower, He is my Fortress, my
4. He is my Prophet, my Priest, and my King, He is my Bread of Life,
5. Je - sus in sor - row, in joy, or in pain, Je - sus my Treas - ure in

Sav - iour is He: Guid - ing, pro - tect - ing, o'er life's roll - ing sea,
com - fort or wealth, Sun - shine or tem - pest, what - ev - er it be,
Strength and my Power; Life Ev - er - last - ing, my Day'sman is He,
Fountain and Spring; Bright Sun of Righteousness, Day - star is He,
loss or in gain; Con - stant Com - pan - ion, wher - e'er I may be,

CHORUS.

Might - y De - liv - 'rer— Je - sus for me. Je - sus for me,
He is my safe - ty:— Je - sus for me.
Bless - ed Re - deem - er,— Je - sus for me.
Horn of Sal - va - tion— Je - sus for me.
Liv - ing or dy - ing— Je - sus for me!

Je - sus for me, All the time, ev - ery - where, Je - sus for me.

Copyright, 1885, by WM. J. KIRKPATRICK.

121. Exhortation. C. M.

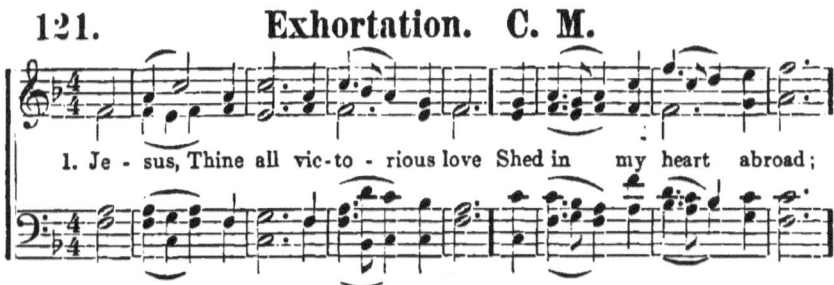

1. Je-sus, Thine all vic-to-rious love Shed in my heart abroad; Then shall my feet no long-er rove, Root-ed and fix'd in God.

2 O that in me the sacred fire
Might now begin to glow;
Burn up the dross of base desire,
And make the mountains flow.

3 O that it now from heav'n might fall,
And all my sins consume;
Come, Holy Ghost, for Thee I call;
Spirit of burning, come.

4 Refining fire, go through my heart;
Illuminate my soul;
Scatter Thy life through every part,
And sanctify the whole.

5 My steadfast soul, from falling free,
Shall then no longer move,
While Christ is all the world to me,
And all my heart is love.

122. O Joyful Sound of Gospel Grace!

1 O joyful sound of gospel grace!
Christ shall in me appear;
I, even I, shall see His face,
I shall be holy here.

2 The glorious crown of righteousness
To me reached out I view;
Conqueror thro' Him, I soon shall seize
And wear it as my due.

3 The promised land, from Pisgah's top,
I now exult to see;
My hope is full, O glorious hope!
Of immortality.

4 With me, I know, I feel, Thou art;
But this cannot suffice,
Unless Thou plantest in my heart
A constant paradise.

5 Come, O my God, thyself reveal,
Fill all this mighty void;
Thou only canst my spirit fill;
Come, O my God, my God!

124. 'Tis so Sweet to Trust in Jesus.

Mrs. Louisa M. R. Stead. W. J. Kirkpatrick, by per.

1. 'Tis so sweet to trust in Je-sus, Just to take Him at His word;
2. O how sweet to trust in Je-sus, Just to trust His cleansing blood;
3. Yes, 'tis sweet to trust in Je-sus, Just from sin and self to cease;
4. I'm so glad I learn'd to trust Thee, Pre-cious Je-sus, Saviour, Friend;

Just to rest up-on His promise; Just to know, "Thus saith the Lord."
Just in sim-ple faith to plunge me 'Neath the heal-ing, cleans-ing flood;
Just from Je-sus sim-ply tak-ing Life and rest, and joy and peace.
And I know that Thou art with me, Wilt be with me to the end.

REFRAIN.

Je-sus, Je-sus, how I trust Him; How I've prov'd Him o'er and o'er,

Je-sus, Je-sus, pre-cious Je-sus! O for grace to trust Him more.

From "Songs of Triumph."

127. I Love Him Far Better.

1 John 4: 19.   F. B. GILLESPIE, by per.

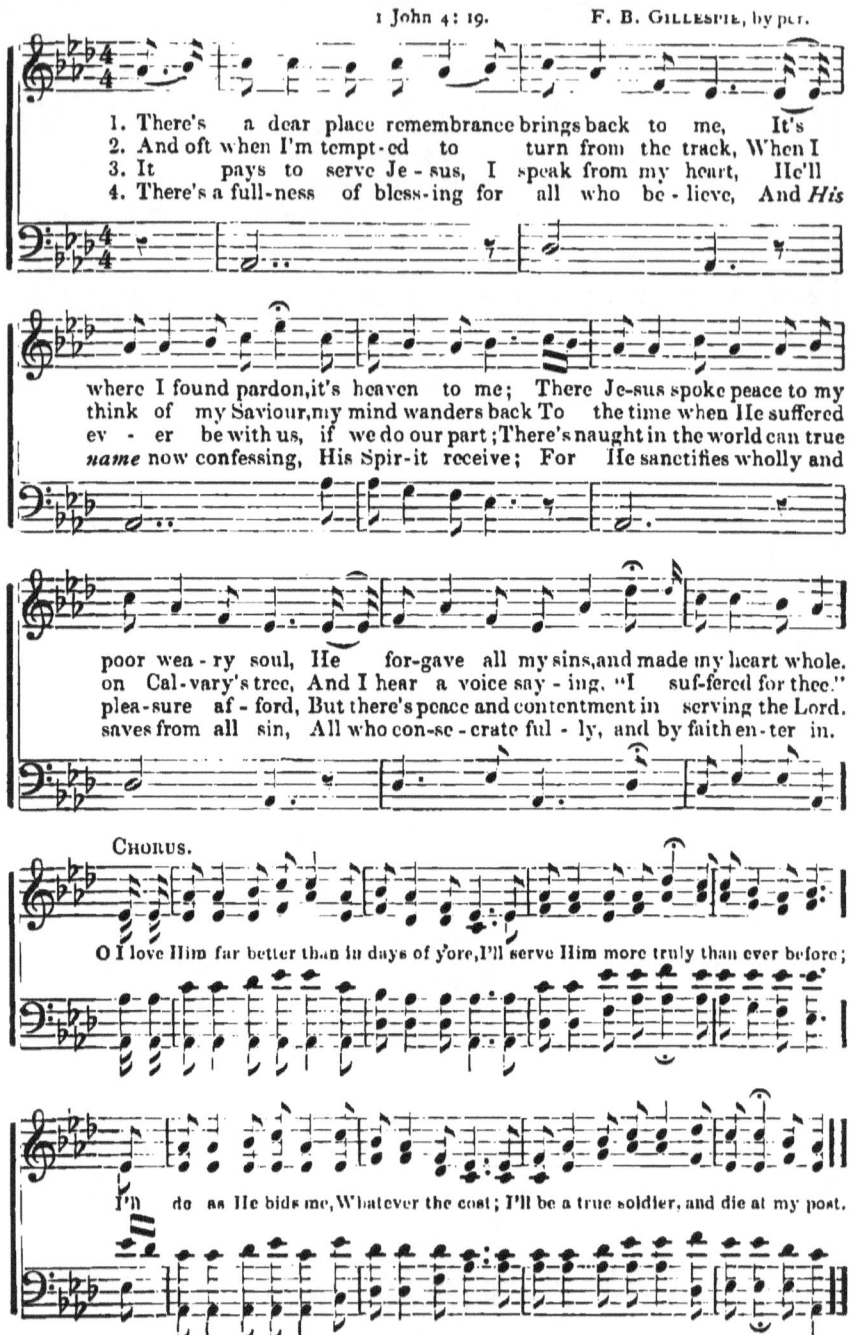

1. There's a dear place remembrance brings back to me, It's where I found pardon, it's heaven to me; There Jesus spoke peace to my poor weary soul, He forgave all my sins, and made my heart whole.
2. And oft when I'm tempted to turn from the track, When I think of my Saviour, my mind wanders back To the time when He suffered on Calvary's tree, And I hear a voice saying, "I suffered for thee."
3. It pays to serve Jesus, I speak from my heart, He'll ever be with us, if we do our part; There's naught in the world can true pleasure afford, But there's peace and contentment in serving the Lord.
4. There's a fullness of blessing for all who believe, And *His name* now confessing, His Spirit receive; For He sanctifies wholly and saves from all sin, All who consecrate fully, and by faith enter in.

CHORUS.

O I love Him far better than in days of yore, I'll serve Him more truly than ever before; I'll do as He bids me, Whatever the cost; I'll be a true soldier, and die at my post.

128. Going Home at Last.

Rev. W. Gossett. E. S. Lorenz.

1. The evening shades are falling, The sun is sinking fast; The Holy One is calling, We're go-ing home at last.
2. The road's been long and dreary, The toils came thick and fast; In body weak and weary, We're go-ing home at last.
3. We now are near-ing heaven, And soon shall be at rest; Our crowns will soon be giv-en, We're go-ing home at last.
4. Oh, praise the Lord for-ev-er, Our sorrows all are past; We'll part no more, no, nev-er, We are at home at last.

Chorus.
Go-ing home at last, Go-ing home at last; The march will soon be over, We're going home at last.

By permission.

129. The Lord's Prayer.

Reverently.

1. Our Father which art in heaven hallowed | be thy | name, ‖ Thy kingdom come, thy will be done in | earth, as it | is in | heaven.
2. Give us this day our | daily | bread, ‖ And forgive us our trespasses, as we forgive | them that | trespass a- | gainst us.
3. And lead us not into temptation, but deliver | us from | evil; ‖ For thine is the kingdom, and the power and the | glory for- | ever and | ever. ‖ A- | men.

130. Face the Other Way.

E. R. Latta.
Frank M. Davis.

1. Broad the road of e-vil, And the crowd is there, Sowing to the whirlwind,
2. What the Lord commandeth, Hear it and o-bey, Ere too late for-ev-er.
3. In the way so nar-row, Where His people go, Let your feet be treading,
4. "Blessed of my Father!" Hear the Saviour say, E'en this moment choose Him,

Lay-ing up despair; If you're in the broad road, Flee from it to-day,
Face the oth-er way; If you're in the broad road, Flee from it to-day,
Sin-ner here be-low; If you're in the broad road, Flee from it to-day,
Face the oth-er way; If you're in the broad road, Flee from it to-day,

D.S.—If you're in the broad road, Flee from it to-day,

FINE. CHORUS.

If you're looking sinwards, Face the oth-er way. Face the oth-er way,
If you're looking sinwards, Face the oth-er way.

D.S.

Face the oth-er way, If you're looking sinwards, Face the oth-er way.

Copyright, 1893, by H. H. Hadley.

131. Standing on the Promises.

R. K. C.   By per. John J. Hood.   R. Kelso Carter.

1 Standing on the promises of Christ my King,
  Through eternal ages let His praises ring;
  Glory in the highest, I will shout and sing,
  Standing on the promises of God.—Cho.

2 Standing on the promises I cannot fail,
  Listening every moment to the Spirit's call,
  Resting in my Saviour, as my all in all,
  Standing on the promises of God.—Cho.

Chorus.

Standing, Standing, Standing on the promises of God my Saviour;
Standing, Standing, I'm standing on the promises of God.

Words and Music in "Precious Hymns." John J. Hood, Pub., Phila.

132. Follow All the Way.

Geo. W. Collins.   Arr. by Wm. J. Kirkpatrick.

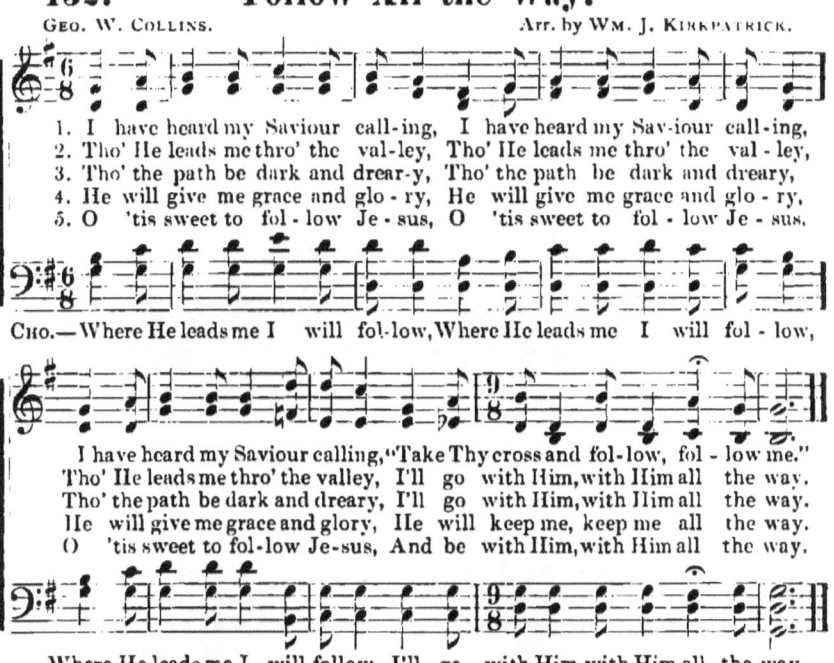

1. I have heard my Saviour call-ing, I have heard my Sav-iour call-ing,
2. Tho' He leads me thro' the val-ley, Tho' He leads me thro' the val-ley,
3. Tho' the path be dark and drear-y, Tho' the path be dark and dreary,
4. He will give me grace and glo-ry, He will give me grace and glo-ry,
5. O 'tis sweet to fol-low Je-sus, O 'tis sweet to fol-low Je-sus.

Cho.—Where He leads me I will fol-low, Where He leads me I will fol-low,

I have heard my Saviour calling, "Take Thy cross and fol-low, fol-low me."
Tho' He leads me thro' the valley, I'll go with Him, with Him all the way.
Tho' the path be dark and dreary, I'll go with Him, with Him all the way.
He will give me grace and glory, He will keep me, keep me all the way.
O 'tis sweet to fol-low Je-sus, And be with Him, with Him all the way.

Where He leads me I will follow, I'll go with Him, with Him all the way.

Copyright, 1891, Wm. J. Kirkpatrick. By per.

133. He Leadeth Me.

J. H. Gilmore.   William Batchelder Bradbury.

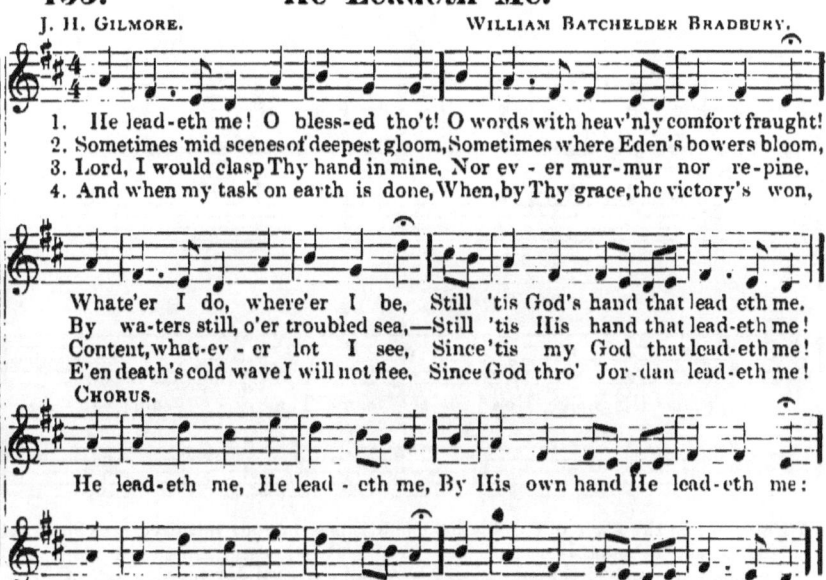

1. He lead-eth me! O bless-ed tho't! O words with heav'nly comfort fraught!
2. Sometimes 'mid scenes of deepest gloom, Sometimes where Eden's bowers bloom,
3. Lord, I would clasp Thy hand in mine, Nor ev-er mur-mur nor re-pine,
4. And when my task on earth is done, When, by Thy grace, the victory's won,

Whate'er I do, where'er I be, Still 'tis God's hand that lead eth me.
By wa-ters still, o'er troubled sea,—Still 'tis His hand that lead-eth me!
Content, what-ev-er lot I see, Since 'tis my God that lead-eth me!
E'en death's cold wave I will not flee, Since God thro' Jor-dan lead-eth me!

Chorus.

He lead-eth me, He lead-eth me, By His own hand He lead-eth me:

His faith-ful follower I would be, For by His hand He lead-eth me.

134. The Very Same Jesus.

L. H. Edmunds.   "This same Jesus."—Acts 1:11.   Wm. J. Kirkpatrick.

1. Come, sin-ners, to the Liv-ing One, He's just the same Je-sus
2. Come, feast up-on the "living bread," He's just the same Je-sus
3. Come, tell Him all your griefs and fears, He's just the same Je-sus
4. Come un-to Him for clear-er light, He's just the same Je-sus

As when He raised the wid-ow's son, The ver-y same Je-sus.
As when the mul-ti-tudes He fed, The ver-y same Je-sus.
As when He shed those lov-ing tears, The ver-y same Je-sus.
As when He gave the blind their sight, The ver-y same Je-sus.

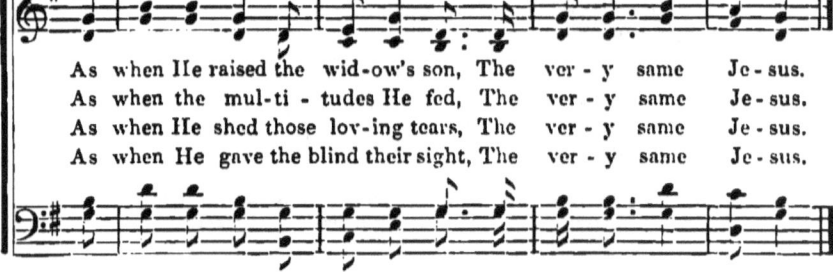

CHORUS.

The ver-y same Je-sus, The won-der work-ing Je-sus;

Oh, praise His name, He's just the same, The ver-y same Je-sus.

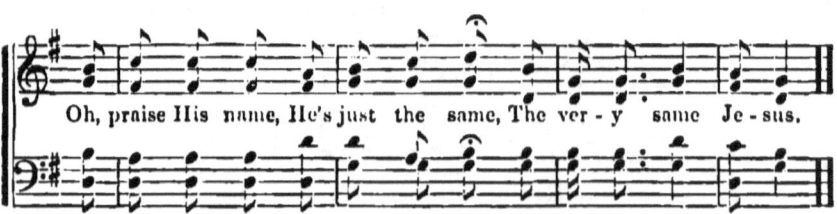

5 Calm 'midst the wave of trouble be,
   He's just the same Jesus
As when He hushed the raging sea,
   The very same Jesus.

6 Some day our raptured eyes shall see
   He's just the same Jesus;
Oh, blessed day for you and me!
   The very same Jesus.

Copyright, 1891, by Wm. J. Kirkpatrick.

135. Tell it Again.

Mrs. M. B. C. Slade. R. M. McIntosh.

1. In-to the tent where a gyp-sy boy lay, Dy-ing a-lone at the close of the day, News of sal-va-tion we car-ried; said he,
2. "Did He so love me,—a poor lit-tle boy? Send un-to me the good tid-ings of joy? Need I not per-ish? my hand will he hold?
3. Bending we caught the last words of his breath, Just as he en-tered the val-ley of death;"God sent His Son!"—"who-so-ev-er?" said he;
4. Smiling, he said, as his last sigh he spent, "I am so glad that for me He was sent!" Whispered, while low sank the sun in the west,

"No-bod-y ev-er has told it to me!"
"No-bod-y ev-er the sto-ry has told!"
"Then I am sure that He sent Him for me!"
"Lord, I be-lieve, tell it now to the rest!"

REFRAIN.

Tell it a-gain! Tell it again? Salvation's sto-ry re-peat o'er and o'er, Till none can say of the children of men,"No-bod-y ev-er has told me be-fore."

By permission.

138. Life's Railway to Heaven.

M. E. ABBEY. CHARLIE D. TILLMAN, by per.
SOLO OR DUET. *Tempo ad lib.* (With or without chorus.)

1. Life is like a mountain railroad, With an en-gi-neer that's brave;
2. You will roll up grades of tri-al; You will cross the bridge of strife;
3. You will of-ten find obstructions; Look for storms of wind and rain;
4. As you roll a-cross the tres-tle, Spanning Jordan's swelling tide,

We must make the run suc-cess-ful, From the cra-dle to the grave;
See that Christ is your Con-duc-tor, On this lightening train of life;
On a fill, or curve, or tres-tle, They will al-most ditch your train;
You be-hold the Un-ion De-pot In-to which your train will glide;

Watch the curves, the fills, the tun-nels; Nev-er fal-ter, nev-er fail;
Al-ways mind-ful of obstruction, Do your du-ty, nev-er fail;
Put your trust a-lone in Je-sus; Nev-er fal-ter, nev-er fail;
There you'll meet our bless-ed Lead-er, God the Fa-ther, God the Son,

Rit.

Keep your hand up-on the throt-tle, And your eye up-on the rail.
Keep your hand up-on the throt-tle, And your eye up-on the rail.
Keep your hand up-on the throt-tle, And your eye up-on the rail.
With the heart-y, joy-ous plau-dit, "Wea-ry pil-grim, welcome home."

CHORUS.

Bless-ed Sav-iour, Thou wilt guide us, Till we reach that bliss-ful shore;

Copyright, 1891, by CHARLIE D. TILLMAN.

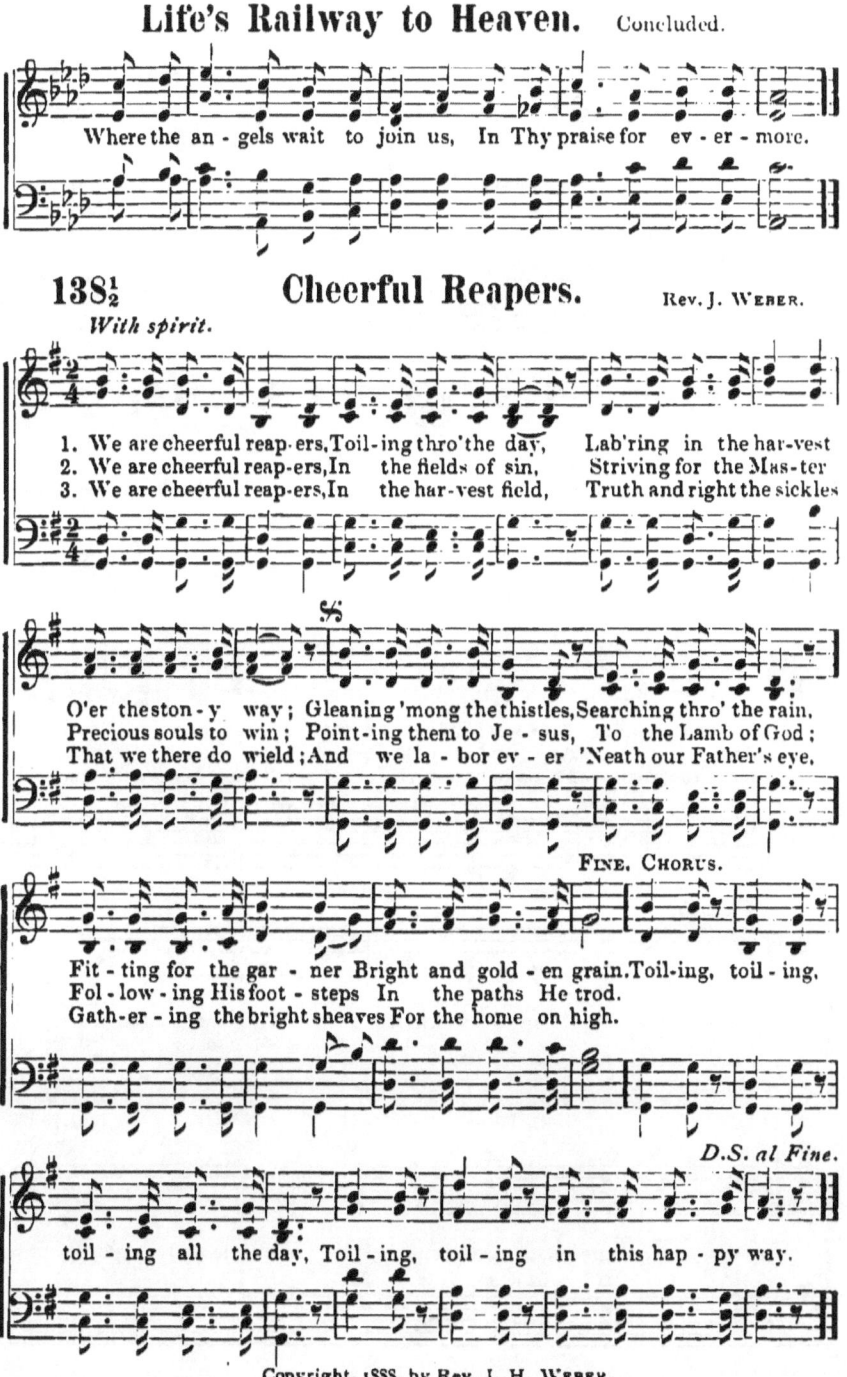

The Palace of the King. Concluded.

3 She cometh to the King
  In robes with needle wrought;
  The virgins that do follow her
  Shall unto Thee be brought.
With gladness and with joy,
  Thou all of them shalt bring,
  And they together enter shall
  The palace of the King.—Cho.

4 And in Thy father's stead,
  Thy children Thou shalt take,
  And in all places of the earth
  Them noble princes make.
I will show forth Thy name
  To generations all:
  The people therefore evermore
  To Thee give praises shall.—Cho

142. At the Fountain.

OLD MELODY.

1. Of Him who did sal-va-tion bring, I'm at the fountain drinking,
   I could for-ev-er think and sing, I'm on my journey home.
2. Ask but His grace, and lo! 'tis given, I'm at the fountain drinking,
   Ask and He turns your hell to heav'n, I'm on my journey home.
3. Tho' sin and sor-row wound my soul, I'm at the fountain drinking,
   Je-sus, Thy balm will make me whole, I'm on my journey home.
4. Where'er I am, where'er I move, I'm at the fountain drinking,
   I meet the ob-ject of my love, I'm on my journey home.
5. In-sa-tiate to this spring I fly, I'm at the fountain drinking,
   I drink and yet am ev-er dry, I'm on my journey home.

CHORUS.

Glory to God, I'm at the fountain drinking, Glory to God, I'm on my journey home.

last verse, My soul is sat-is-fied.

143. The Master Stood in His Garden.

"We have this treasure in earthen vessels."—2 Cor. 4:7.

E. R. V. Dedicated to Mr. and Mrs. Dr. F. W. Owen. JAMES McGRANAHAN.

1. The Mas-ter stood in His gar-den, A-mong the li-lies so fair,
2. "My li-lies have need to be wa-tered," The heaven-ly Mas-ter said:
3. But the Mas-ter saw and raised it From the dust in which it lay,
4. So forth to the fountain He bore it, And filled it full to the brim;
5. The droop-ing li-lies He wa-tered, Till all re-viv-ing a - gain.
6. And then to it - self it whispered, As a-side He laid it once more.

Which His own right hand had plant-ed, And trained with ten-d'rest care;
"Where-in shall I draw it for them, And raise each droop-ing head?"
And smiled as He gent-ly whis-pered, "My work it shall do to - day;
How glad was the earth-en ves-sel To be of some use to Him!
The Mas-ter saw with pleas-ure His la-bor had not been in vain;
"I still will lie in His path - way, Just where I did be - fore;

He looked at their snow-y blos-soms, And marked, with ob-serv-ant eye,
Close, close to His feet on the path-way, All emp-ty, and frail, and small,
It is but an earth-ern ves-sel, But close it is ly-ing to Me;
He poured forth the liv-ing wa-ter All o-ver His li-lies so fair,
His own hand drew the wa-ter, Re-fresh-ing the thirst-y flowers;
For close would I keep to the Mas-ter, And emp-ty would I re - main,

That His flowers were sad-ly drooping For their leaves were parched and dry,
Was an earth-ern ves-sel ly-ing, That seemed of no use at all,
It is small, but clean, and emp-ty,— That is all it needs to be,
Till emp-ty was the ves-sel, And a - gain He filled it there,
But He used the earth-ern ves-sel To con-vey the liv-ing showers,
Per-chance some day He may use me To wa-ter His flowers a - gain.

Copyright, 1884, by James McGranahan. Used by purchase of right.

The Master Stood in the Garden. Concluded.

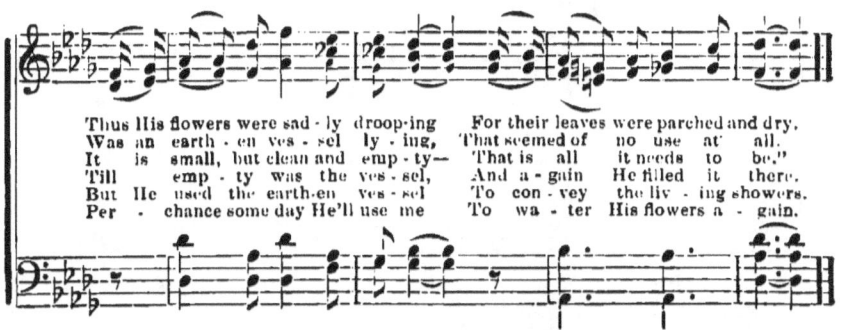

Thus His flowers were sad-ly droop-ing For their leaves were parched and dry.
Was an earth-en ves-sel ly-ing, That seemed of no use at all.
It is small, but clean and emp-ty— That is all it needs to be."
Till emp-ty was the ves-sel, And a-gain He filled it there.
But He used the earth-en ves-sel To con-vey the liv-ing showers.
Per-chance some day He'll use me To wa-ter His flowers a-gain.

144. May I Know Thy Voice.

HENRY H. HADLEY.   John 17:3.   AZMON.

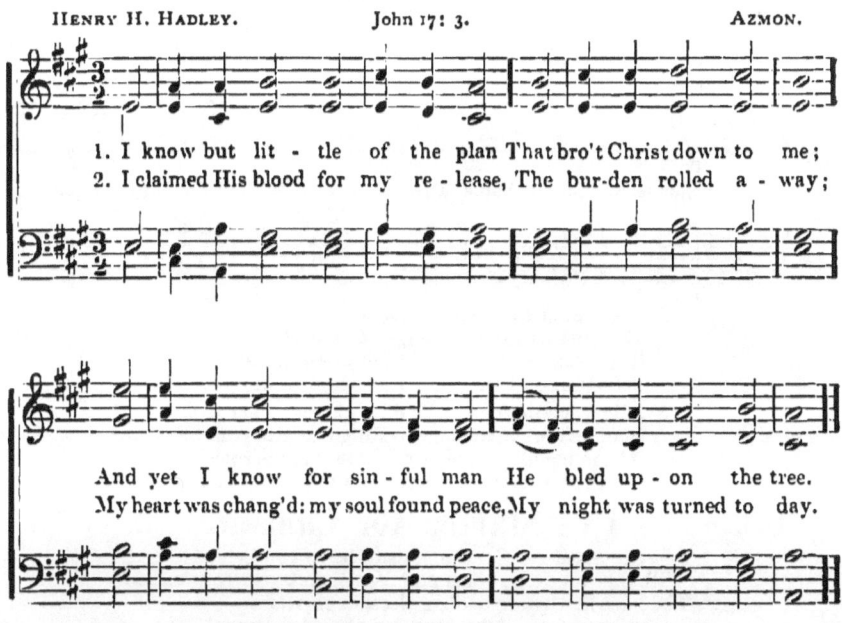

1. I know but lit-tle of the plan That bro't Christ down to me;
And yet I know for sin-ful man He bled up-on the tree.
2. I claimed His blood for my re-lease, The bur-den rolled a-way;
My heart was chang'd: my soul found peace, My night was turned to day.

3 This much, my simple heart doth know,
   The witness lives within;
   To others I will quickly go,
   Their precious souls to win.

4 No Greek or Hebrew can I speak,
   Nor learned questions scan;
   But when He speaks I know His voice:
   For Jesus talks with man.

5 So I will all my life employ
   To tell the story sweet,
   That Jesus saves from drink and sin,
   And makes my life complete.

6 I'll not grow cold while winning them,
   To give but helps my store;
   For every one I bring to Christ,
   I love Him more and more.

Copyright, 1892, by H. L. GILMOUR.

145. The Saint's Home.

Words by DAVID DENHAM.　　Music from a German Melody.

1. 'Mid scenes of con-fu-sion and creature complaints,
   How sweet to my soul is com-(*Omit* . . .) munion with saints!
   To find at the banquet of mercy there's room,
   And feel in the presence of (*Omit* . . .) Je-sus at home.

CHORUS.
Home, home, sweet, sweet home! Prepare me, dear Saviour, for glory, my home!

2 The pleasures of earth I have seen fade away;
They bloom for a season, but soon they decay;
But pleasures more lasting in Jesus are given,
Salvation on earth, and a mansion in heaven.—*Cho.*

3 Allure me no longer, ye false glowing charms!
The Saviour invites me—I'll go to His arms:
At the banquet of mercy I hear there is room;
O! there may I feast with His children at home.—*Cho.*

146. I've Started for Canaan.

1 I have started for Canaan, must I leave you behind?
Will you not go up with me? come, make up your mind:
The land lies before us, 'tis pleasant to view;
Its fruits are abundant, they are offered for you.
　　Come, come, friends, friends, come,
　　I've started for Canaan, oh, will you not come?

2 What can tempt you to linger, or turn from the way?
The fields are all blooming, as blooming as May:
The music is charming, the harmony pure;
The joys there are lasting, they ever endure.—*Come, etc.*

3 'Tis the last call of mercy, oh! turn, lest you die!
Give your heart to the Saviour, to-day He is nigh:
While His arms are extended, while His children all pray,
Will you not join our number? come, join us to-day.—*Come, etc.*

147. Nearer the Cross.

"The Cross of our Lord Jesus Christ." Gal. 6: 14.

FANNY J. CROSBY.   MRS. J. F. KNAPP. By per.

1. "Near-er the cross!" my heart can say, I am com-ing near-er, Near-er the cross from day to day, I am com-ing near-er; Near-er the cross where Je-sus died, Near-er the fountain's crim-son tide, Near-er my Saviour's wounded side, I am com-ing near-er, I am com-ing near-er.

2. Near-er the Christian's mer-cy seat, I am com-ing near-er, Feasting my soul on man-na sweet, I am com-ing near-er; Stronger in faith, more clear I see Je-sus who gave him-self for me; Near-er to Him I still would be, Still I'm com-ing near-er, Still I'm com-ing near-er.

3. Near-er in pray'r my hope aspires, I am com-ing near-er, Deep-er the love my soul de-sires, I am com-ing near-er; Near-er the end of toil and care, Near-er the joy I long to share, Near-er the crown I soon shall wear: I am com-ing near-er, I am com-ing near-er.

148. Where is my Father To-night?

CARRIE MERRES.   Air.—"Where is my Wandering Boy?"

1 Where has my father gone to-night?
The father I love so well;
He wanders away from home and friends;
My sorrow no words can tell.

CHO.—O where is my sire to night?
O where can my father be?
I love him yet, I cannot forget
My mother's last words to me.

2 Once we could say our home was bright,
As we knelt at his knee for prayer;

No face more kind, no heart more true—
None loved us with fonder care.—CHO.

3 I stood and watched by her dying bed,
And softly she said to me,
"I feel that our prayers will yet be heard;
Your father reclaimed will be."—CHO.

4 Go to my wandering sire to-night,
And tell him the words of love,
That I may hope we'll meet again
On earth, or with mother above.—CHO.

Copyright, 1890, by H. H. HADLEY.

149. We're on the Way!

S. M. SAYFORD.   Isaiah 35: 8-10.   D. B. TOWNER, by per.

1. The promised land! by faith I see, Where God's own glo-ry gilds the day,
2. The promis'd land! where thousands dwell, Who've wash'd their robes in Jesus' blood,
3. The promised land! with gates of pearl, A-jar for all the blood-wash'd throng.
4. The promised land! with mansions fair, Where Je-sus now prepares a place.
5. The promised land! the Father's house A-waits us on the shin-ing shore,

Where we shall dwell with Christ redeem'd, By His own grace we're on the way.
With them we'll wave the branch of palm, When we have cross'd the narrow flood.
A few more marches—hold on faith! And then we'll sing Redemption's song,
From whence He'll come to take us home, And we shall see Him, face to face.
When there we'll strike our harps of gold, And praise His name for-ev - er-more.

CHORUS.

We're on the way, we're on the way, To glo - ry-land, we're on the way;

We fol-low Je-sus day by day, He leads us all a - long the way.

By permission of D. B. TOWNER, owner of Copyright.

150. At the Cross.

ISAAC WATTS.   **R. E. HUDSON.**

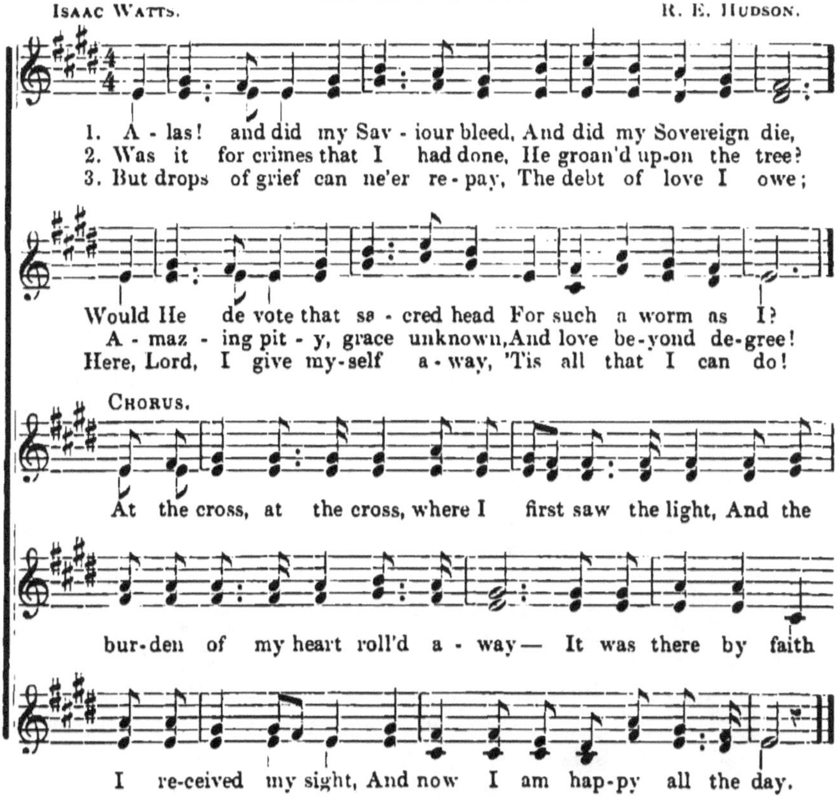

1. A-las! and did my Sav-iour bleed, And did my Sovereign die,
2. Was it for crimes that I had done, He groan'd up-on the tree?
3. But drops of grief can ne'er re-pay, The debt of love I owe;

Would He de-vote that sa-cred head For such a worm as I?
A-maz-ing pit-y, grace unknown, And love be-yond de-gree!
Here, Lord, I give my-self a-way, 'Tis all that I can do!

CHORUS.

At the cross, at the cross, where I first saw the light, And the bur-den of my heart roll'd a-way— It was there by faith I re-ceived my sight, And now I am hap-py all the day.

Copyright. 1865, by R. E. HUDSON.

151. Oh, How I Love Jesus!

JOHN NEWTON.

[*Omit in Repeat......*]

CHORUS.

[*Omit in Repeat......*]

1 How sweet the name of Jesus sounds
In a believer's ear!
It soothes his sorrows, heals his wounds,
And drives away his fear.

CHO.—|| : Oh, how I love Jesus! : ||
    Because He first loved me ;
|| : How can I forget Thee? : ||
    Dear Lord, remember me.

2 It makes the wounded spirit whole,
And calms the troubled breast ;
'Tis manna to the hungry soul,
And to the weary rest.

3 I would Thy boundless love proclaim
With every fleeting breath ;
So shall the music of Thy name
Refresh my soul in death.

152. My Jesus, I Love Thee.

London Hymn Book.
A. J. Gordon.

1. My Jesus, I love Thee, I know Thou art mine, For Thee all the follies of sin I re-sign; My gracious Redeemer, my Saviour art Thou, If ever I loved Thee, my Jesus, 'tis now.
2. I love Thee, because Thou hast first loved me, And purchased my pardon on Calvary's tree; I love Thee for wearing the thorns on Thy brow; If ever I loved Thee, my Jesus, 'tis now.
3. I will love Thee in life, I will love Thee in death, And praise Thee as long as Thou lendest me breath; And say when the death-dew lies cold on my brow, If ever I loved Thee, my Jesus, 'tis now.
4. In mansions of glory and endless delight, I'll ever adore Thee in heaven so bright; I'll sing with the glittering crown on my brow, If ever I loved Thee, my Jesus, 'tis now.

By permission.

153. Come, Ye Disconsolate.

T. Moore.
11, 10.

1. Come, ye disconsolate, where'er ye languish, Come to the mercy-seat, fervently kneel; Here bring your wounded hearts, here tell your anguish; Earth has no sorrow that Heav'n cannot heal.

2 Joy of the desolate, light of the straying,
  Hope of the penitent, fadeless and pure,
  Here speaks the Comforter, tenderly saying,
    "Earth has no sorrow that Heaven cannot cure."

3 Here see the bread of life; see waters flowing
  Forth from the throne of God, pure from above;
  Come to the feast of love; come, ever knowing
   Earth has no sorrow but heaven can remove.

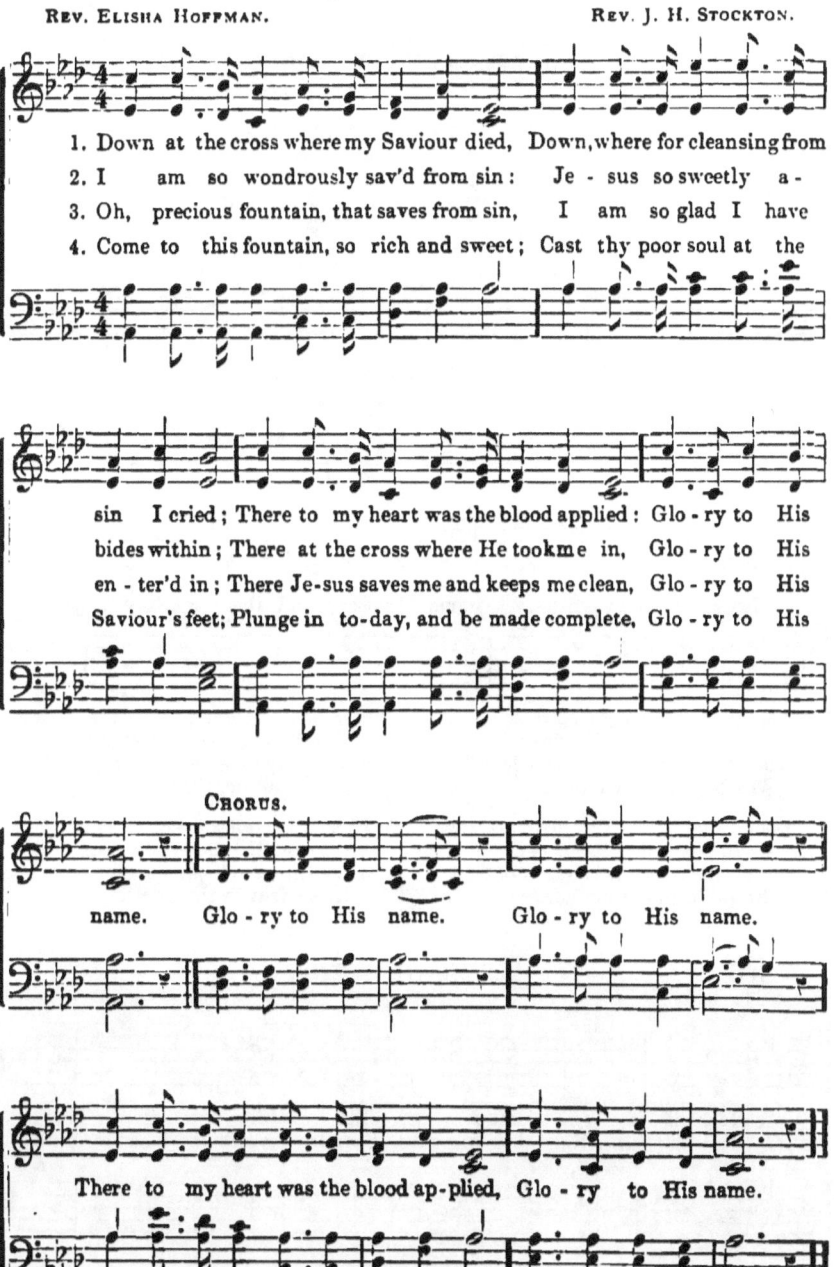

155. There is a Fountain.

W. COWPER.   LOWELL MASON.

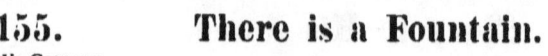

1. There is a foun-tain filled with blood, Drawn from Im-man-uel's veins,
And sin-ners plung'd beneath that flood Lose all their guilt-y stains.
Lose all their guilt-y stains Lose all their guilt-y stains;

2 The dying thief rejoiced to see
That fountain in his day;
And there may I, though vile as he,
Wash all my sins away.

3 Dear dying Lamb, Thy precious blood
Shall never lose its power,
Till all the ransomed church of God
Be saved to sin no more.

4 E'er since, by faith, I saw the stream
Thy flowing wounds supply,
Redeeming love has been my theme,
And shall be, till I die.

5 Then in a nobler, sweeter song,
I'll sing Thy power to save,
When this poor lisping, stam'ring tongue
Lies silent in the grave.

156 Rock of Ages.

A. TOPLADY.   Tune—TOPLADY. 7s.

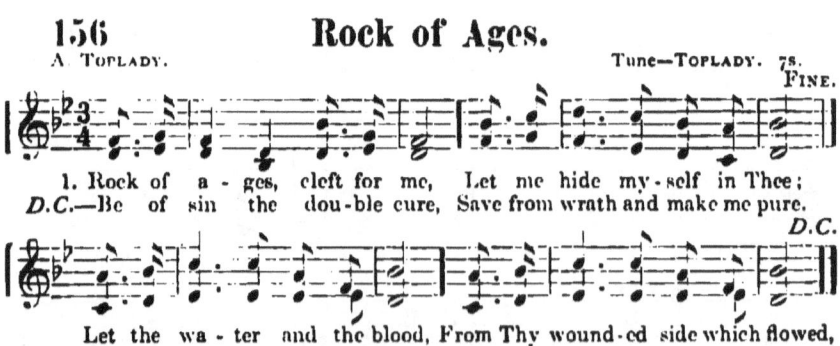

1. Rock of a-ges, cleft for me, Let me hide my-self in Thee;
D.C.—Be of sin the dou-ble cure, Save from wrath and make me pure.
Let the wa-ter and the blood, From Thy wound-ed side which flowed,

2 Could my tears forever flow,
Could my zeal no languor know,
These for sin could not atone;
Thou must save, and Thou alone:
In my hand no price I bring;
Simply to Thy cross I cling.

3 While I draw this fleeting breath,
When my eyes shall close in death,
When I rise to worlds unknown,
And behold Thee on Thy throne,
Rock of ages, cleft for me,
Let me hide myself in Thee.

157. Awake, My Soul.

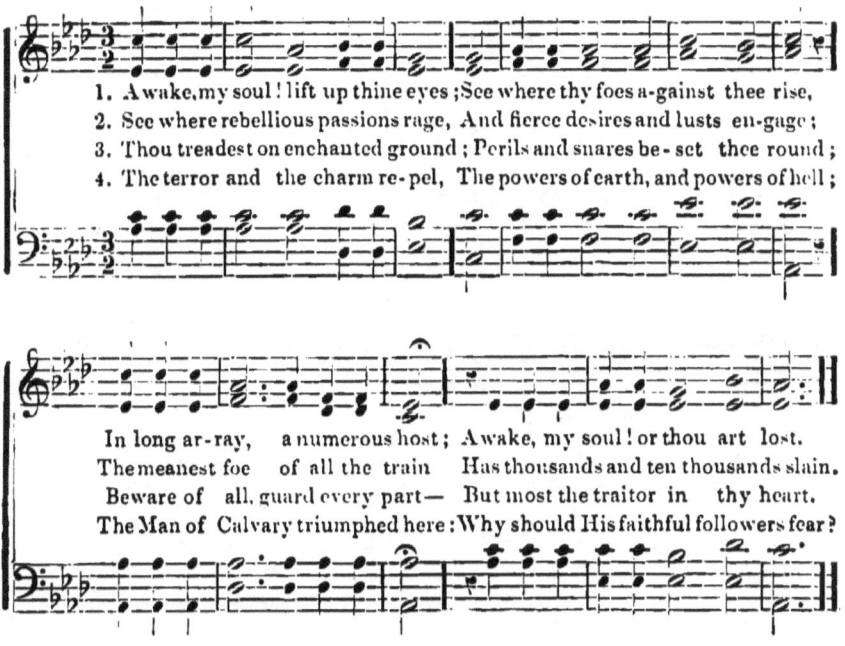

1. Awake, my soul! lift up thine eyes; See where thy foes a-gainst thee rise,
In long ar-ray, a numerous host; Awake, my soul! or thou art lost.

2. See where rebellious passions rage, And fierce desires and lusts en-gage;
The meanest foe of all the train Has thousands and ten thousands slain.

3. Thou treadest on enchanted ground; Perils and snares be-set thee round;
Beware of all, guard every part— But most the traitor in thy heart.

4. The terror and the charm re-pel, The powers of earth, and powers of hell;
The Man of Calvary triumphed here; Why should His faithful followers fear?

158. My God, My Father, While I Stray.

1 My God, my Father, while I stray
Far from my home, on life's rough way,
Oh, teach me from my heart to say,
"Thy will be done, Thy will be done!"

2 What though in lonely grief I sigh
For friends beloved no longer nigh;
Submissive still would I reply,
"Thy will be done, Thy will be done!"

3 If Thou should'st call me to resign
What most I prize—it ne'er was mine,
I only yield thee what was Thine:
"Thy will be done, Thy will be done!"

4 If but my fainting heart be blest
With Thy sweet Spirit for its guest,
My God, to thee I leave the rest;
"Thy will be done, Thy will be done!"

5 Renew my will from day to day;
Blend it with Thine, and take away
Whate'er now makes it hard to say,
"Thy will be done, Thy will be done!"

6 Then when on earth I breath no more,
The prayer oft mixed with tears before
I'll sing upon a happier shore:
"Thy will be done, Thy will be done!"

159. Dear Lord, Amid the Throng.

1 Dear Lord, amid the throng that pressed
Around Thee on the cursed tree,
Some loyal, loving hearts were there,
Some pitying eyes that wept for Thee.

2 Like them may we rejoice to own
Our dying Lord, tho' crown'd with thorn;
Like Thee, Thy blessed self, endure
The cross with all its cruel scorn.

3 Thy cross, Thy lonely path below,
Show what Thy brethren all should be;
Pilgrims on earth, disowned by those
Who see no beauty, Lord, in Thee.

161. Gathering Home.

Miss MARIANA B. SLADE.   R. N. M'INTOSH. By per.

1. Up to the boun-ti-ful Giv-er of life,—Gathering home! gathering home!
2. Up to the city where falleth no night,—Gathering home! gathering home!
3. Up to the beautiful mansions above,—Gathering home! gathering home!

Up to the dwelling where cometh no strife, The dear ones are gathering home.
Up where the Saviour's own face is the light, The dear ones are gathering home.
Safe in the arms of His in-fin-ite love, The dear ones are gathering home.

CHORUS.

Gath-er-ing home!......... gath-er-ing home!.........
Gath-er-ing home!   gath-er-ing home!

Nev-er to sorrow more, never to roam; Gathering home!
                                                            Gath-er-ing home!

gath-er-ing home!   God's chil-dren are gath-er-ing home.
               gath-er-ing home!

162. I Have Tried the World.

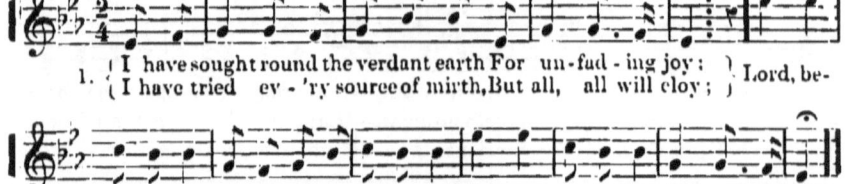

1. { I have sought round the verdant earth For un-fad-ing joy;
   { I have tried ev-'ry source of mirth, But all, all will cloy; } Lord, bestow on me Grace to set my spirit free; Thine the praise shall be, Mine, mine the joy

2 I have wandered in mazes dark
  Of doubt and distress;
 I have had not a kindling spark,
  My spirit to bless;
 Cheerless unbelief
 Filled my lab'ring soul with grief;
 What shall give relief?
  What shall give peace?

3 Then I turned to Thy gospel, Lord,
  From folly away;
 Then I trusted Thy Holy Word
  That taught me to pray;

Here I found release—
 In Thy Word my soul found peace,
 Hope of endless bliss,
  Eternal day.

4 I will praise now my heavenly King,
  I'll praise and adore;
 All my heart's richest tribute bring
  To Thee, God of power;
 And in heaven above,
 Saved by Thy redeeming love,
 Loud the strains shall move
  For evermore.

163. I'll Live For Him.

C. R. DUNBAR.

1. My life, my love I give to Thee, Thou Lamb of God, who died for me:
2. I now be-lieve Thou dost re-ceive. For Thou hast died that I might live;
3. Oh, Thou who died on Cal-va-ry, To save my soul and make me free,

CHO.—I'll live for Him who died for me, How hap-py then my life shall be!

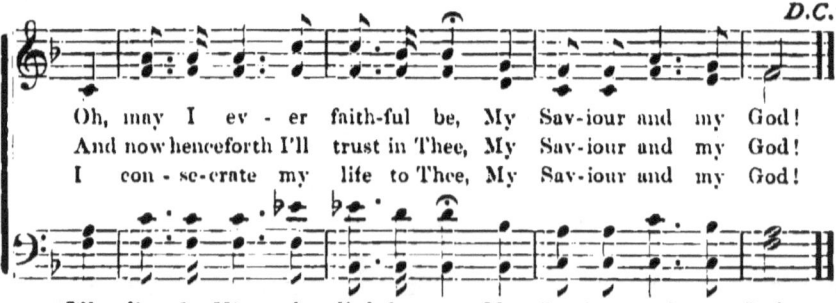

Oh, may I ev-er faith-ful be, My Sav-iour and my God!
And now henceforth I'll trust in Thee, My Sav-iour and my God!
I con-se-crate my life to Thee, My Sav-iour and my God!

I'll live for Him who died for me, My Sav-iour and my God.

By permission.

164. Stand up for Jesus.

G. DUFFIELD.   G. J. WEBB.

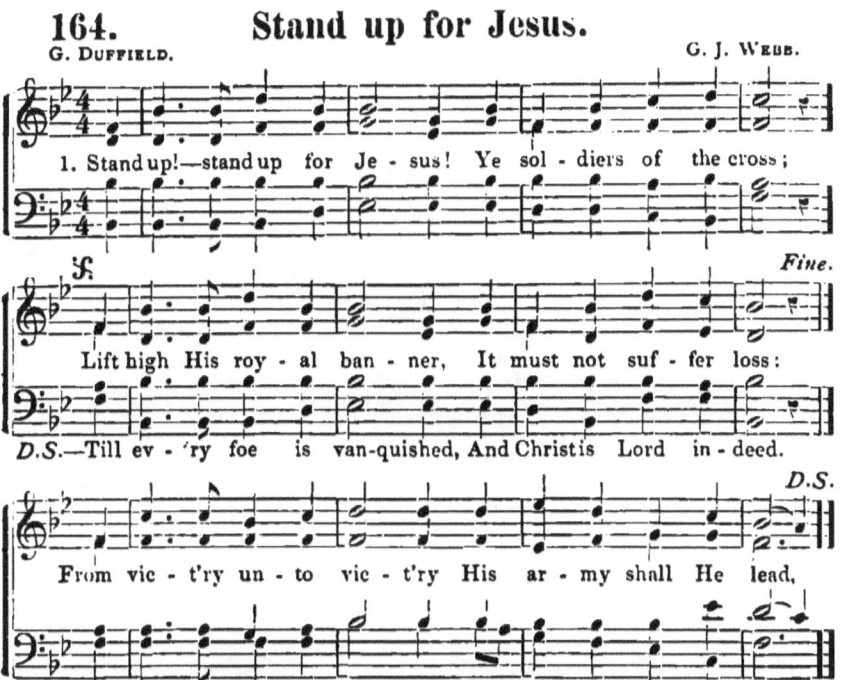

1. Stand up!—stand up for Jesus! Ye soldiers of the cross;
Lift high His royal banner, It must not suffer loss:
From vict'ry unto vict'ry His army shall He lead,
Till ev-'ry foe is vanquished, And Christ is Lord indeed.

2 Stand up!—stand up for Jesus!
  The trumpet call obey;
Forth to the mighty conflict,
  In this His glorious day:
"Ye that are men, now serve Him,"
  Against unnumbered foes;
Let courage rise with danger,
  And strength to strength oppose.

3 Stand up!—stand up for Jesus!
  The strife will not be long;
This day, the noise of battle,
  The next, the victor's song:
To him that overcometh,
  A crown of life shall be;
He with the king of glory
  Shall reign eternally!

---

1 The morning light is breaking;
  The darkness disappears!
The sons of earth are waking
  To penitential tears;
Each breeze that sweeps the ocean
  Brings tidings from afar,
Of nations in commotion,
  Prepared for Zion's war.

2 See heathen nations bending
  Before the God we love,
And thousand hearts ascending
  In gratitude above;

While sinners, now confessing,
  The gospel call obey,
And seek the Saviour's blessing—
  A nation in a day.

3 Blest river of salvation!
  Pursue thine onward way;
Flow thou to every nation,
  Nor in thy richness stay:
Stay not till all the lowly
  Triumphant reach their home:
Stay not till all the holy
  Proclaim—"The Lord is come!"
                S. F. SMITH.

---

1 From Greenland's icy mountains,
  From India's coral strand,
Where Afric's sunny fountains
  Roll down their golden sand,—
From many an ancient river,
  From many a palmy plain,
They call us to deliver
  Their land from error's chain.

2 Waft, waft, ye winds, His story,
  And you, ye waters, roll,
Till, like a sea of glory,
  It spreads from pole to pole;
Till o'er our ransomed nature,
  The Lamb, for sinners slain,
Redeemer, King, Creator,
  In bliss returns to reign.

165. Sweet By-and-By.

S. FILLMORE BENNETT.   JOS. P. WEBSTER, by per.

1. There's a land that is fair-er than day, And by faith we can see it a-far; For the Fa-ther waits o-ver the way, To prepare us a dwell-ing-place there.
2. We shall sing on that beau-ti-ful shore The mel-o-di-ous songs of the blest, And our spir-its shall sor-row no more, Not a sigh for the bless-ing of rest.
3. To our boun-ti-ful Fa-ther a-bove, We will of-fer our trib-ute of praise, For the glo-ri-ous gift of His love, And the blessings that hal-low our days.

CHORUS.

In the sweet by-and-by, We shall meet on that beau-ti-ful shore, In the sweet by-and-by, We shall meet on that beau-ti-ful shore.

Used by permission of OLIVER DITSON & Co., owners of Copyright.

167. Trust and Obey.

Rev. J. H. Sammis.   D. B. Towner.

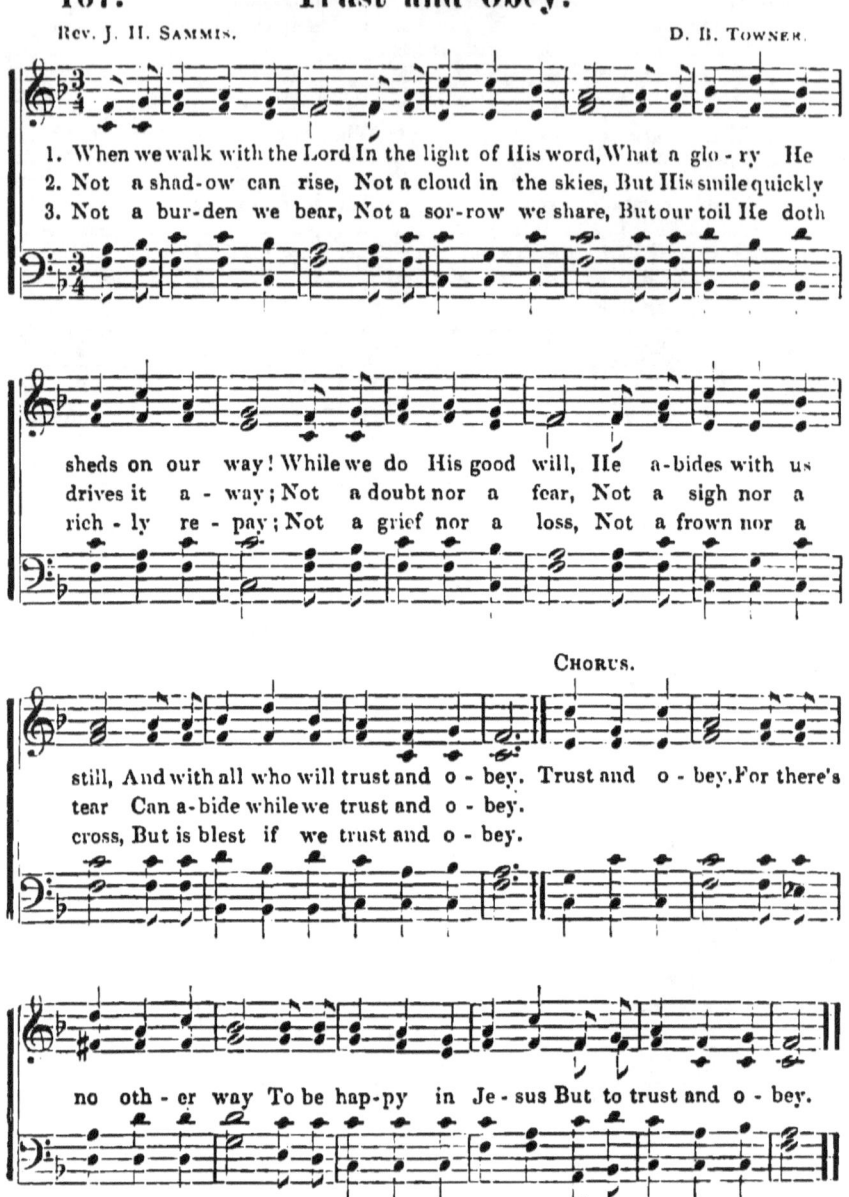

1. When we walk with the Lord In the light of His word, What a glo-ry He sheds on our way! While we do His good will, He a-bides with us still, And with all who will trust and o-bey.
2. Not a shad-ow can rise, Not a cloud in the skies, But His smile quickly drives it a-way; Not a doubt nor a fear, Not a sigh nor a tear Can a-bide while we trust and o-bey.
3. Not a bur-den we bear, Not a sor-row we share, But our toil He doth rich-ly re-pay; Not a grief nor a loss, Not a frown nor a cross, But is blest if we trust and o-bey.

CHORUS.

Trust and o-bey, For there's no oth-er way To be hap-py in Je-sus But to trust and o-bey.

4 But we never can prove
The delights of His love
Until all on the altar we lay,
For the favor he shows,
And the joy He bestows,
Are for all who will trust and obey.

5 Then in fellowship sweet
We will sit at His feet,
Or we'll walk by His side in the way;
What He says we will do,
Where He sends we will go,
Never fear, only trust and obey.

Copyright, 1887, by D. B. Towner. Used by per.

170. Blessed Assurance.

"He is faithful that hath promised."—HEB. 10: 23.

F. J. CROSBY.　　　　　　　　　　　MRS. JOSEPH F. KNAPP. By per.

1. Bles-sed as-sur-ance, Je-sus is mine! O, what a fore-taste of glo-ry di-vine! Heir of sal-va-tion, pur-chase of God, Born of His Spir-it, wash'd in His blood.
2. Per-fect sub-mis-sion, per-fect de-light, Vis-ions of rapt-ure now burst on my sight. An-gels de-scend-ing bring from a-bove, Ech-oes of mer-cy, whis-pers of love.
3. Per-fect sub-mis-sion, all is at rest, I in my Sav-ior am hap-py and blest, Watch-ing and wait-ing, look-ing a-bove, Fill'd with His good-ness, lost in His love.

CHORUS.

This is my sto-ry, this is my song, Prais-ing my Sav-ior all the day long; This is my sto-ry, this is my song, Prais-ing my Sav-ior all the day long.

Copyright, 1873, by JOSEPH F. KNAPP.

INDEX TO HYMNS.

	No.
All for sinners	104
A little talk	43
All taken away	88
And wilt Thou yet be found	107
Anywhere with Jesus	139
Are you washed in the blood	160
Arise, my soul, arise	97
A shout in the camp	4
At even ere the sun was set	86
At the cross	150
At the fountain	142
Awake, my soul	157
Bear the cross for Jesus	36
Behold the Bridegroom	26
Behold the man	82
Blessed assurance	170
Blest be the tie that binds	119
Blow ye the trumpet, blow	97
Burst, ye emerald gates	3
Can a boy forget his mother?	114
Cheerful reapers	138½
Christ is all	87
Cleansing fountain	71
Consecration	105
Come thou fount of every blessing	110
Come to the Saviour	40
Come, ye disconsolate	153
Dear Jesus, canst Thou help me	67
Dear Lord, amid the throng	159
Decide to-night	89
Diamonds in the rough	166
Down in the gilded saloon	94
Drifting away	57
Face the other way	130
Fill me now	56
Flash the toplights	12
Follow all the way	132
From every stormy wind that blows	63½
From Greenland's icy mountains	164
Gather them in	112
Gathering home	161
Give me a heart like thine	102
Give me Jesus	81
Glory to God! hallelujah	48
Glory to his name	154
God be with you	68
God's word	14
Going home at last	128
He is able to deliver thee	111
He is calling	57½
He is just the same to-day	55
He leadeth me	133
He saves the drunkard too	113
Holy Spirit, faithful guide	85
How firm a foundation	7
How vain are all things here below	113
I am bound for the kingdom	103
I have tried the world	162
I know thou art praying for me	92
I'll bear it, Lord, for Thee	100
I'll feed on husks no more	64
I'll live for Him	163
I love him far better	127
I love to tell the story	23
I'm believing and receiving	99
I'm going back to Jesus	93
I'm kneeling at the mercy-seat	118
In Canaan now	66
In evil long I took delight	109
Into his fold	11
I stood outside the gate	60
I stretch my hands to Thee	65
Is not this the land of Beulah?	30
I thirst, Thou wounded Lamb of God	86
It will never grow old	125
I've started for Canaan	146
I will shout His praise in glory	41
Jesus bids you come	35
Jesus for me	120
Jesus shall reign	5
Jesus, the light	62
Keep close to Jesus	58
Keep moving on the way	59
Lead me gently home, Father	34
Lead me, Saviour	61
Leaning on the everlasting arms	136
May I know Thy voice	144
Mercy is boundless and free	70
Move forward	9
My country! 'tis of thee	10
My faith looks up to Thee	10
My God, my Father, while I stray	158
My happy home	19
My Jesus, I love Thee	152
My son, give Me thy heart	20
Nearer, my God, to thee	16

INDEX TO HYMNS.

Title	No.
Nearer the cross	147
Now I feel the sacred fire	63
O could I speak the matchless worth	1
O happy day	22
Oh, how I love Jesus	151
Oh, how sweet at Jesus' feet	18
Oh, such wonderful love	126
O joyful sound of gospel grace	122
On the cross of Calvary	116
Onward, Christian soldiers	137
O turn ye, O turn ye	106
Place a lamp in the window	72
Power in Jesus blood	17
Praise God from whom all blessings	86
Realms of beauty	108
Redeemed	33
Rejoice and be glad	27
Rejoice! the lost is found	53
Rest and home	91
Revive us again	28
Rock of Ages	156
Roll on the gospel chariot	84
Safe within the vail	51
Saved to the uttermost	171
Shall I turn back	69
Since I have been redeemed	77
Sing the story	96
Sowing the tares	54
Standing on the promises	131
Stand up for Jesus	164
Step out on the promise	74½
Sunshine in the soul	98
Sweetly resting	93½
Sweet peace, the gift of God's love	75
Tell it again	135
Tell it to Jesus alone	123
The beautiful city of gold	45
The best friend is Jesus	140
The Comforter has come	50
The child of a King	31
The cross	38
The general roll call	15
The glorious hope	74
The gospel feast	13
The great Physician	2
The half was never told	49
The happy pilgrim	29
The Jericho service	47
The Lord's prayer	129
The Lord will provide	39
The Master stood in His garden	143
The new "over there"	169
The old time religion	115
The palace of the King	141
The pilgrim company	24
The prodigal's return	42
The Rock that is higher than I	46
The sinner's home	145
The song of jubilee	90
The stranger at the door	44
The very same Jesus	134
There is a fountain	155
There's a great day coming	95
This is the life line	52
This just suits me	168
Thus far the Lord hath led me on	6
Though your sins be as scarlet	73
Throw out the life line	52
'Tis so sweet to trust in Jesus	124
Trust and obey	167
You had better make your peace	83
Vain man, forbear	79½
Wave the signal light	76
Welcome for me	25
We'll never say good by	101
We're on the way	149
We walk by faith	21
What shall the harvest be?	79
What's the news	80
Where is my father to-night	148
Where the living waters flow	8
Whiter than snow	78
Why I love Jesus	117
Wonderful love of Jesus	32
Wonderful story of love	37

www.ingramcontent.com/pod-product-compliance
Lightning Source LLC
Chambersburg PA
CBHW030304170426
43202CB00009B/861